YANKEES REMEMBER...

HOW IT USED TO BE

Edited by
Clarissa M. Silitch

Designed by
Carl F. Kirkpatrick

Foreword by
Newton F. Tolman

Published MCMLXXVI
by Yankee, Inc., Dublin, New Hampshire, 03444

First Edition

Copyright 1976 by Yankee, Inc.

All rights reserved including the right to reproduce
this book, or parts thereof, in any form, except for
the inclusion of brief quotations in a review

•

ISBN 0-911658-69-6

Library of Congress Catalog Card No. 76-16337

Manufactured in the United States of America

CONTENTS

Foreword *by Newton F. Tolman*	6
Dashing Through the Snow *by Henry M. Plummer*	8
Watching Grandmother Dress *by Margaret Waterman*	16
The Prose of Hunting Bees *by Alfred Stevens*	20
Oh, to be Young Again and at Wesleyan Grove *by Howard G. Wilson*	24
Here Come the Elephants *by Floyd Lee Bell*	32
Diary of a Real Schoolteacher *by Amy G. Jarvis*	34
Canoeing on the Charles *by Arthur F. Joy*	46
The Moxie Team *by Edna Hills Humphrey*	52
Down by the Depot *by Stephen S. Bean*	56
Towels with Tassels and Oh, That View *by Edith Mason*	62
Covered Wagons in the Yard *by Margo Holden*	74
A Rigorous and Gentle Art *by John Chase*	76
Salt Hay *by Ned Brown and Frank W. Lovering*	82
The Hub of the Universe *by Frances Minturn Howard*	84
Waste Not, Want Not *by Pauline L. Jensen*	94
Better Than Walking *by John H. Ackerman*	96
A Golden Era *by Manley H. Grant*	102
The Philosopher's Animal *by Norman Myrick*	110
That You Mabel? *by Haydn S. Pearson*	116
The Yard *by Florence B. Jacobs*	118
Magic on Main Street *by Albert G. Miller*	122
Slowest of the Slow *by William H. Sanders*	134
A Day on the Kennebec *by L. B. Woodward*	136
Getting There Was Half the Fun *by Stephen Alexander*	142
The Glorious Fourth *by Irwin Ross and Melvin Haugan*	146
Iron Character and Where It Came from *by Claire W. Reed*	148
Last of Its Kind *by Ernest H. Cole*	156
Rolling the Roads *by Henry N. Andrews, Jr.*	158
Bubble, Bubble, Sing and Stir *by Eliza St. Clair*	164
Why It's Like You're Right There! *by Paul J. Reale*	166

FOREWORD

Writers and publishers often tangle in rather heated debate about just what is meant by "regional writing." Usually the publisher is trying to explain why the writer's wares couldn't succeed outside his home town. But the unfortunate writer is always sure that, like Faulkner's novels or Frost's poetry, his work will have a wide appeal *because* of its regional character.

From the time when Robb Sagendorph started working on the first issue of *Yankee*, a one-room shoestring operation in his own house, he never doubted that the magazine would some day make it on the national scene. For the next twenty-five years it was a hard constant struggle, but Robb refused to listen to the magazine experts who thought he was attempting the impossible. No regional, country-type magazine, they said, had ever got beyond a strictly local circulation.

By the 1960s, Robb had surprised himself. When I ran into him early one morning over at Larry's garage (he was dragging an oily, grimy old shaft from the garage dump — just the thing for his newest bird feeder, save him a trip to Keene — and I helped him load it into the trunk of the new Continental) he said something like, "Sometimes these days I just can't believe what *Yankee* has grown into — it seems as though it must be a dream!" I said, "Well, it was — back in 1935. Remember?"

What we were really talking about was that *Yankee*, at long last, had proved that there were many people in Texas, in Alaska, in England, or wherever, who could be more fascinated by our own little corner of the U.S. and its authentic rural history, than some native New England readers themselves.

Endless evidence of this now comes to mind, in part from "fan mail." Fan mail, to a writer or an editor, is as much a part of the work-a-day world as it is to a movie actor, politician, or Red Sox hero.

My favorite example of a *Yankee* magazine fan appeared three or four years ago, up here on our remote mountainside, at the not-very-beguiling hour of 7 A.M. A sturdy old gentleman of eighty or so, he had collected all my books and New England writings and brought them to be signed, which I was flattered to do.

He told us he was a retired dairy farmer from near Lancaster, Pennsylvania; had never been in New England before, but had become an ardent collector of New England lore largely from reading *Yankee*. (I guess it's the only magazine he ever reads.) He might be upset if I used his real name here; it is Pennsylvania Dutch, and sounds something like Carl B. Haystacker.

When my wife served Carl coffee, he took some cream from a small pitcher, then looked at her sternly and remarked, "Hm, such heavy cream, it's extravagant, you know!"

When he had finished his coffee and accepted a few things I gave him for his collection, he said he must be going, as he planned to drive the whole way before evening. And he asked how he could start off by way of Dublin, as he wanted to see the *Yankee* building. It was the only shrine in New England he was interested in visiting.

Carl has written me once or twice a year ever since. One typically laconic communication contained only, "You have not had anything in *Yankee* now for more than one year. Why? — Sincerely yours, Carl B. Haystacker." I felt properly rebuked. And every Christmas, he sends me a *Yankee* gift subscription . . . "To save you from having to spend the money yourself."

For the New Anglophiles, wherever they may be, the pictures and text between these covers will offer an entertaining view of our history roughly spanning 1890-1940.

Among the many unusual pieces I was glad to see preserved in book form, one about ice-cutting strikes a special note. Maybe because, in younger days, I was privileged to work a couple of weeks every winter harvesting several tons of pond ice on the farm — an interesting occupation, especially in fine, favorable ice weather; around zero, with a brisk wind howling across the pond, and the ever-present challenge of not slipping into ten-foot-deep arctic water.

Even here in New England, few youngsters of today, at least those under forty-five, are hardly aware of this once vast and vital industry; and that it employed a shipping business the length of the eastern coast and even to foreign ports. When electricity reached the rural areas, ice harvesting disappeared as suddenly as our old kerosene parlor lamps and barn lanterns. Doubtless now, with a return to natural energy becoming a national obsession, some of those learning about natural-ice refrigeration as it once was, will start taking a second look at it.

This book, however, is more a social journal than a history. It is like going down the road to an old cellar-hole of a house long gone, and finding for a moment it has reappeared, and some old-timer inside is there to tell you a yarn about how things used to be.

Newton F. Tolman
Nelson,
New Hampshire

A smart brush on County Street.

Courtesy The Whaling Museum, New Bedford, Massachusetts.

🍃 SLEIGHING 🍃

Dashing Through the Snow

by Henry M. Plummer

Every kind of sleigh ever built was in that throng. Doubles and singles and old-fashioned bathtubs with screaming eagles or red roses painted on the back. Plumes waved ... furs trailed ... bells tinkled on shafts and harnesses.

The boys of New Bedford, Massachusetts, did not go to the wharves to begin their boating experiences until they were 12 years old at least. But sitting in their parents' laps they held the reins over old Dobbin from the day they were five. In the 1870s our townsfolk recognized the horses at a distance, just as they recognized the well-known citizens.

The roan cob heading up Bush Street, now Madison Street, on the dead run would be pulling Captain Delano home to his dinner, and the Captain would have the reins round his neck and be reading the paper while the buggy lurched from side to side and spun the corners on two wheels or one runner. Captain Delano had commanded a clipper ship—or was it a Liverpool packet?—and knew not fear in a buggy. Everybody else did, however, and at that certain time of day Bush Street was always free and clear for the Charge of the Light Brigade.

Anybody could tell Charlie Fleetwood on the box of his hack from half a mile away by the two little bay horses, with a star on the forehead of the off horse. A New Bedford hack was an institution similar to a hearse built for four, and it harbored a smell all its own. Passengers changed often, but that smell never; and dusty, musty, all-pervading, it was the first glad welcome home to a returning traveller.

In sleighing time the city demonstrated its love for horses on County Street; at about two o'clock could be heard the merry jingle of the bells on every street as each horse and sleigh was bound for County Street between Union Street and Washington Square.

On bright, sunny, snapping cold afternoons the city gave itself to snow carnival and the horse was king.

No young fellar could hope to hold love and affection if he failed to take her sleigh-riding on County Street. What a jolly sight it was, and what a merry time they had! A gay scene bright with color, happy faces, cheerful laughter, and constant movement.

If, in the excitement, your horse had not run away, you turned around in Washington Square and walked single file up County, while watching the passing show on its prancing way towards the Square.

Every kind of sleigh ever built was in that throng. Doubles and singles and old-fashioned bathtubs, with pictures of screaming eagles or baskets of red roses painted on the back. Plumes waved from the dash boards, furs trailed from the seats, bells tinkled on shafts and on leather straps circling the horses. The slow ones kept on the west side on the way down, and the speeders raced the middle as tight as they could go.

We always had one or two horses that could turn a smart brush on the road, and my father was very fond of sleighing. They wrapped me round with a robe in the house, and carried me like a little mummy to the sleigh where I was again tucked snugly in beside my father.

Everybody in town was on the street, either in the sleighs or in the crowd that lined the sidewalks, and we all knew each other and knew all the horses and just how fast each could go.

John S. Cook drove a good one, and so did Ebsen Perry and his son, Ned. Captain Joe Ricketson from Clarks Point always had a fast one. Bob Snow drove Cassius, a wild-eyed, big-gaited horse ever at the point of running away and often doing it. Bill Nye, in a high-backed bathtub with a picture on the back, held the reins over a funny-looking nag that might have found a cow perched on some spreading limb of her family tree, but could scramble down the hills at quite a clip. Walter Thornton drove a roan, and David Snell had Lady Snell between the shafts, while Bill Richards often led the bunch with a pacer. Some days Mr. Rotch drove Trump, but Morgan Rotch held the reins more often and skillfully guided the little horse to almost certain victory.

How well I remember the picture from a little south of Bedford Street as we walked slowly north. The first cry from the crowded sidewalks "Here they come! Here they come!" The bunch of racing horses leaping into sight, half hidden in the swirling snow and rushing down the hill. As they drew nearer, the crowd could pick the leaders and shout its joy.

"Richards is ahead! No, he ain't, it's Lady Snell! My money on Cassius if Bob can hold him!"

Then from the whirling bunch you might see the head of a little mouse-colored horse, weaving its way in and out wherever a gap offered a chance. Trotting with level head, ears forward, and guided by a master hand, Trump would push to the front and the crowd, quick to sense the skill and effort, would change its cry and cheer to "Trump is coming through! Watch Trump! See him come! Drive him, Morg! He wins, Trump wins!" and away they dash with snow flying, whips waving, drivers yelling, crowd screaming, horses trotting, some running, all carried away with an ecstasy of joyful excitement.

Accidents of a serious nature were practically unknown, which spoke louder for the intelligence of the horses than for the skill of the drivers. I can remember but one mishap in the many years I sleighed on County Street. Old man Waterman, the auctioneer, without looking behind, pulled up short at the foot of the Bedford Street hill, and coming fast with no chance to turn, we struck him full and by. The

The armory now stands on the site of the handsome Cory house in New Bedford. Mr. A. Davis Ashley and his wife are in the sleigh drawn by this pretty team of pinto ponies.

Courtesy Free Public Library, New Bedford, Massachusetts.

poor old man wrapped in his blanket sailed in the air, and describing a perfect parabolic curve, landed on his head and shoulder in the roadway. Father, picking up hat and wig on the way, ran to help him when the good old sport snatched the wig and jammed it into his pocket saying, "Damn the wig and the old fool who wore it where he shouldn't have been." One shoulder was dislocated and Father drove him to Job Sweet, the skillful bone-setter, who snapped it back into place. From then until Waterman could no longer fish the streams, he sent us every spring a fine basket of trout.

This was sleighing on County Street in the early '70s. Laying of the Bedford Street car track spoiled the racing on that part of the street, and the sleighers, moving farther south, raced from Washington Square to River Street. Faster horses appeared and the racing became a more determined feature. Gradually the friendly, neighborly rivalry gave way to semiprofessional earnestness, and the joy went out of the game.

I cannot leave the story of New Bedford sleighing without mentioning one more incident, although it happened many years later.

Morgan Rotch had the rare fortune to drive the two fastest horses that ever trotted County Street to sleigh. After Trump's day, he bred and raised the bay mare Phantom, a high-stepping, noble-looking horse of surprising speed on the snow for a short distance.

John Rhodes determined to beat Phantom and bought several horses with that particular end in view, yet year after year the laurels still went to Rotch's gallant mare. Then the snow came again, and there was talk of Rhodes and a pacer, and there were whisperings of excitement to come. I am all horse as I write and am going into some detail, for there still may be some readers of this story who will remember that afternoon and remember Phantom too.

She was a high-gaited horse that could show her speed in any footing, be it smooth as a table or knee deep in slush and snow. She had the winning ability of leaping almost from a walk into her full stride, and she had a skillful driver who knew her every fault and virtue, and who could carry her to a break and with the turn of his wrist settle her back to a trot without loss

Another New Bedford equipage. The driver could well be a retired sea captain.

Courtesy The Whaling Museum, New Bedford, Massachusetts.

This photo was snapped on County Street, New Bedford, just north of Union Street, in the days of the flannel-wrapped brick foot-warmers.

Courtesy Free Public Library, New Bedford, Massachusetts.

of the least speed. It was well known that Phantom lacked stamina, and could never trot the full mile at speed, but the County Street course of half a mile or less suited her exactly. It was doubted if she had the courage to make a good stern chase, but she never had to try, for, together with the skill of her driver and her quick starting facility, she was always away in the lead.

There came an afternoon when the footing was hard, smooth, and just suited for the pacers. Rhodes brushed his horse down the stretch a few times, and Rotch let Phantom warm to her stride alone. I pulled up just north of River Street, blanketed my horse, and waited with the crowd to see the finish. There was the silence of tense expectancy and an occasional excited voice jarred on your nerves in the still cold winter's air.

How I wish you might get but a small part of the picture now in my mind. The golden light of the afternoon sun shining on that smooth white roadway, flashing on the brightly painted sleighs, blue, red, yellow, and green. Flashing on the glistening furs, the gay hats, bright colored coats, brass-mounted harness, and on the silver of tinkling bells. Far up the street the two long colorful lines converged at the bend in a misty iridescent sheen.

Then the far-away murmur throbbing to the steady roar of the voice of the excited multitude as, rounding the turn, racing horses sprang into view. On they came with Phantom well in the lead, head high and hoofs pounding out the rhythm of flying speed. The pacer behind but now fairly settled to his stride was racking side for side with machine-like power, and closing up the gap faster and faster. As they drew nearer we could see Phantom's flaring red nostrils opened wide in search of air for laboring lungs. She plainly showed the effects of strain and, as the pacer's head lapped by his sleigh, Rotch pulled Phantom back, and Rhodes bore by like a whirlwind.

The race was over and it was all fair for they had reached the point where slowing down was permissible. The home favorite had won and the crowd was happy, but there were 200 yards of open road ahead and had they raced another 50, Phantom would have lost a crown.

Another little yarn that has a dash of comedy to it, and then I am done with horses, sleighs, and County Street.

One season I had no horse to burn a burst of speed, and drove from Potomska to stand on the sidewalk and watch the racing, which was almost as much fun as racing yourself. One afternoon I noticed a shaggy-coated little horse, hitched to a heavy milk pung, but trotting fast and in a manner that showed she was born to the purple. Next morning I drove to town early and found the milkman up Mt. Pleasant way. I bought his horse for a small sum, and led her behind my sleigh to Andrew Hathaway's blacksmith shop to have her clipped, for she looked more like a Skye terrier than a horse. Sleighing days were busy ones for the horse clippers, and it was two o'clock before they began on my nag. Three o'clock came and I could stand it no longer, so had the clipping machine make a straight run from ears to tail, and hitched up my new purchase, with one side clipped to mouse length, and the other with hair as long as a bear. What a good afternoon I did have, and how I did puzzle the crowd which thought at first that I was changing horses at the end of the road. Then what laughter when they discovered the real facts, and how they did cheer the little horse as she footed to a bunch of racers!

I named her "One-eyed Katie, the Milkman's Pride" and I only raced her that one afternoon, for besides being blind in one eye she had a bone disease on her forelegs which caused her great pain when backing and turning around. She could trot and how she did love to go, but to get her pointed up the road again I had to drive her around the whole block.

She paid for herself on that one joyous afternoon, and I took her home for gentle driving only, and kept her for many years which I think she enjoyed, and, when suffering came, a merciful bullet sent her where good brave little horses go.

Now that's all about horses, and I can't add a sketch because the more horses I draw the more they look like pigs; but I can't help wondering if the two hours passed in the stuffy atmosphere of a movie theatre is a good substitute for a winter's afternoon of keen excitement spent in the nipping air on the County Street of those wonderful days of long ago. END

Watching Grandmother Dress

Grandmotherly costumes for a summer's day, circa 1890.

"She's up!" I shout at my sister, who is still asleep. In seconds we have thrust back the covers, struggled into our bathrobes and slippers and are on our way down the hall.

"Quick . . . under the covers," Grandmother W. says, as we burst in. So we kick off our slippers and snuggle obediently under the dark red puff. No make-believe, no fooling around—we don't want to miss a single minute of the show. Grandmother will soon commence the daily ritual of getting dressed. In less than an hour we will have to get dressed too, but not in anything that bears the faintest resemblance to the fascinating garments we will watch her put on. We must drag on long-sleeved undershirts, long-legged underdrawers, nasty little waists with yellowish buttons put on with a bit of tape, stringy garters that dangle down to catch up black, ribbed stockings . . . white stockings on Sundays. The worst part is poking

BUSTLES AND BOWS

No make-believe, no fooling around — we don't want to miss a single minute of the show. *by Margaret Waterman*

Courtesy Elliot Allison.

and yanking the buttons through the buttonholes of the bloomers that match our dresses. Nobody, my mother tells us, likes to see little girls' white panties. So we treat adult lookers to an exhibition of colored bloomers whenever we ride the arms of chairs or swing on porch rails.

Some day, I tell myself as I flatten the silky puff down on my chest for a better view, I won't have to wear these dreadful things. I'll have money of my own, and with it I'll buy underclothes like my grandmother's. Not like my mother's! Hers come in fewer pieces, and they go on much too fast.

We're usually snug under the puff for the very beginning of the show. Although she says the room is too cold for us, Grandmother is walking around laying her clothes on the chairs when we arrive. She is wearing a copious gown of white muslin with ruffles around the neck

17

and the wrists. Her hair is still in curlers, and a wispy gray pigtail hangs down her back.

The first few moments of her reverse strip-tease are tantalizing, for they take place inside her nightgown. We imagine but are never allowed to see the delicate Victorian shifting of shirts that takes place there. Cotton nightgowns, she says, are much too scratchy; so winter and summer alike she wears under her nightgown an old shirt—she always called it a vest—so soft and thin that it is only months from the ragbag. The signal for the beginning of the show is the disappearance of Grandmother's fingers up into her sleeves. A few seconds later we know she has wiggled out of her old vest, for she pokes it out from under her nightgown with her toes. Then she apparently pulls the day vest up over her legs inside the great balloon of nightgown. When it gets up as far as her knees, we see her elbows pushing against the nightgown. "A circus tent, a circus tent!" we shout, remembering the elephants we saw bumping against the canvas tent last summer as they waited for the circus to begin.

By the time the tent has opened, my grandmother is neatly covered almost to her knees by a ribbed cotton vest with short sleeves. A taller grandmother would have been more exposed; this one was less than five feet tall. Now she reaches for her corsets, the article of clothing I most covet. I can hardly take my eyes from them—they are so complicated, so strong, so well equipped, with their hooks and sturdy garters. Sometimes she unties and adjusts the long white lacing that crisscrosses up her back. We watch admiringly as she sucks in her stomach; and I suck mine in under the puff. But the puff is so puffy and I am so little that it doesn't even move. Grandmother W. expertly swings the two stiff pieces of corset around her and begins fitting the little metal eyes over the little metal bumps that run up the front, being careful not to ensnare her vest. (It's a quarter-century to zippers!) She pulls her vest down neatly, and it hangs out like a little skirt below her corsets. Then she reaches for her drawers—not panties, not bloomers, but *drawers*. (I know that bloomers had been invented—I wore them—but my grandmother still favored umbrella drawers. Each leg of her drawers was a large cotton tube trimmed with lace and rows of tiny tucks. The two legs were sewed together only down the front; and it was clear even to little girls of our age that they were meant to be worn only by ladies who sat discreetly on the seats of chairs.) Grandmother's drawers fasten just as her petticoats do, with a narrow tape run through a casing at the top and tied with a safe, double-knotted bow.

Next she puts on her corset-cover, which should have a different name, for it covers only the very top of her corsets. It too is cotton, a bit full, with built-up shoulders, a round neck and a front opening. The tapes—or strings—allow her to distribute the fullness at the neck and at the waist. There is usually scalloped embroidery around the neck and the armholes. She is beginning to look really splendid now.

At this point she puts on her stockings—long, black lisle hose rolled carefully up on her legs to make contact with her wide white garters. Like ours, her garters are elastic, but they are so much more powerful, so much more elegant! The hardware is larger too, and more impressive. The front garters she leans forward to fasten. The side ones she leans slightly to the side to do. But the best ones are the back ones; to fasten them she has to put one hand behind her and the other between her legs. It's a marvellous trick. I know because I've practiced standing that way. And when I play grown-up I always wear corsets with six garters which need frequent fastening.

It's time now for petticoats, two of them—one short and one long. In winter, the short one, which comes only to her knees, is flannel; in summer it matches her corset-covers with ruffles around the bottom. The second one comes to her ankles. She wears a muslin or a sateen one with ruffles sewed on the lower six or eight inches on weekdays. On Sundays she wears a watered taffeta petticoat which shows two different colors and when she walks makes the most elegant swishing sound I have ever heard. I resolve beneath the puff to be rich enough when I grow up to wear a watered taffeta petticoat every day.

By the time the second petticoat is fastened—sometimes with snaps, sometimes with two sets of strings, one of which ties in front and one in back—the show is almost over. But her hair must be combed before she puts on her dress and

A somewhat later grandmother — 1910? 1912?

her shoes. (I think her hair must have been in a state of experiment during the years I remember, for I have mixed recollections of the next act of the show. I remember a *transformation* in the earliest days. This too she tied on with a tape. Then when it was securely fastened around her head, she began brushing it straight down over her face, always remembering to part it like curtains and say something funny as we giggled under the red puff. She then rolled it over some sort of *rat* into the kind of austere hairdo that I have come to associate with Amy Lowell. Later there was a *switch* which was twisted with her own hair into a figure eight.) The mornings I remember best are those when she is wearing what are called electric curlers, though there is nothing electric about them. They make her look as if she has tight-twisted little tails all over her head. Sometimes she wears kid-curlers that make little snails all over her head. No matter how she combs her hair, this act always ends up with a chase for an elusive gray hairnet which she vows she put under the hand-painted hair-receiver the night before. Once in a while it goes as far astray as the bed, and then we blow on it to see it float along the red puff.

To put her shoes on she sits down on a chair. I don't remember her using the silver-handled buttonhook on the marble-topped bureau. I remember playing with it, but I picture her lacing up high, black shoes—oxfords in summer—which she eased on with a shoehorn from Hamilton & Butterfield's. I always raise my head to see if she is skipping any holes or forgetting to cross to the other side. But her lacing is always without fault. When I am old enough to use a shoehorn, I tell myself, I probably won't miss holes either.

Just before the dress comes the final bit of splendor: the bust ruffle. It's a gay deceiver, so to speak, worn by flat-chested women in an age when cleavage is of no concern to the wearer or the public either. It is a series of over-hanging strips of lace gathered and sewed onto a rectangle of net. The whole thing stands out at least an inch beyond the corset-cover. And the bust-ruffle is unique in my grandmother's wardrobe in that it doesn't tie; it has to be pinned to her corset-cover with little gold safety pins. Each day it offers a new challenge. It calls for experiment and scrutiny; it inspires her to back away from the mirror and cock her head first on one side and then on the other.

Except for her dress, she is now ready to face the world—and a marvellous sight she is. I don't remember her dresses—except that on Sunday she wore silk foulards fitted out with such contraptions by her dressmaker that the whole family had to lay hooks to eyes and pop snaps on metal humps to get her to church on time. (Her dresses I did not covet. I aspired to freedom in my elegance. And I strongly suspect that what I was hoping to wear fifteen or twenty years later was already quite old-fashioned as I nestled envious under the red puff.)   END

Starting off on a wild honey hunt, bee box in hand.

WILD HONEY

The Prose of Hunting Bees
by Alfred Stevens

...to discover just where, in some old hollow trunk, those canny insects had hoarded up their golden treasure.

As soon as late summer fields outcropped with nuggets of goldenrod, a spare, Yankee figure was sure to appear at the open doorway of the old family workshop. At once Father and I knew what was in the wind. Clad in khaki from head to foot, with laced-up canvas leggings equal to all the tangled briers in the countryside, Uncle Buzz was in dress rehearsal for the season of the bee hunt. He might be fondling his homemade catch box, skillfully built of walnut and fitted with brass springs and slides. Perhaps it had some slight improvement, added since last fall, to lead into the subject of the day. Failing that, the blooming of the goldenrod, or the lovely weather itself, or the busy hum of bees surveying the grapevine over the shop door would serve as well. No matter what the approach, the three of us were already of one mind, eager to go.

Then out came the gear for inspection, cleaning, and any small repair that might be in order. Next, to choose the day and starting point. Finally, to fit the bee box with a fresh comb of honey and make sure our own lunches were in preparation. Dawn; dressing for the woods; crew and equipment loaded into the great old touring car; and on to the hunt!

Our route was simply out of town, into the vast stretch of uncut woods and scattered fields in those days sparsely pierced by winding, sandy roads. Leaving the car deep in one of these byways, we were off through trees and brush, ferns, thorns, and bogs, over rocks and ledges and the ever-present stone walls of New England. From the first few steps I was lost, but Father and Uncle, familiar with the countryside from youth, and each wearing a compass at his belt, always seemed to know when we crossed the boundary of Newt LeBaron's eastern patch, or which way lay the rise of Roast Meat Hill or the depth of Bedbug Hollow.

Perhaps it was the shortness of my young legs that made it seem a long and weary trek before we burst upon the sunlit spread of some large field, deep with wild grass and flowers, fragrant with nameless perfume. Here, far from neighboring trees, we gladly dropped our luggage and made ready for the first stand.

Either man with his tackle could have performed the hunt alone. Two made for sociability and added accuracy in observing the homing flight of the bees. I served only as a mascot and auxiliary watcher.

Separated by 50 yards or more, the two hunters put up almost identical equipment, although each had made his own to individual taste. A pole about five and a half feet tall was stood upright by thrusting into the ground a spike attached to its lower end. At its top was fastened the bee box, about an inch and a half larger in every dimension than the commercial square comb of honey that it contained. The box was of wood, with a wooden lid hinged to open to the right. Under this was a glass lid hinged to open to the left. With both lids open, the top of the honeycomb would be exposed to the air.

In one side of the box was a hole just large enough for a bee to go through, but blocked by a metal slide closed by a spring. So stood the box, then, with both lids shut, completely dark inside.

Now each hunter went forth to find his first bee, plying her trade calmly on a flower. We always took Italians, for they were the best workers in our country. The bee, and often part of the flower, were snapped up in the catch box, a sort of square wooden mouth hinged along one edge, of a size just to fit comfortably in the hand. Like the bee box, it had a hole in one side, closed by a slide. Held open by a mild spring, the box could be brought close to the unsuspecting bee, then quickly put over her head and shut. A self-acting catch held it closed, and the prisoner suddenly found herself in darkness, for the joints of the box were lightproof.

Then the catch box was taken to the bee box and attached to its side by means of an ingenious latch. When the connection was fully made, the holes in the sides of both boxes were automatically aligned together and their slides both opened, so the bee could pass through to the honeycomb if she wished. We usually gave her a minute or so to calm down in her confinement and then gently opened the wooden lid of the bee box. Seeing the sunlight, our little guest soon made the passage toward it, but found herself contained by the glass lid—on a huge, luscious supply of ready-made honey! In such a case, she did what any sensible working girl would do: she settled down to make the most of it. Observing this cautiously from a wide angle, we then opened the glass lid with great care not to disturb her; and our contact was established.

The next step was of double importance to us: to notice both the time and direction of her departure. The time was not difficult, for she was the sole object of our interest at this period. But the direction was not always so clear. After her recent confusion, the tiny aviator would tend to dart hither and yon before executing the characteristic grand ascending spiral, ending in a sudden, swift tangent as she struck a beeline for home.

The lapsed time until her return gave us a rough idea of how far we were from the hive. Almost invariably, companions would come back with the first bee (if not, we caught and started a second). These, in turn, brought others, so that normally we soon had a continuous procession pointing the direction to their residence as they darted off from the top of their spiral ascent. In due course we would shut the bee box's lid while a group were working, then pick up all our gear and make a march along the indicated bearing. Setting up in another field, we would release our unwilling passengers again and once more study their flight.

Sometimes Uncle Buzz (whose bee-like name was really contracted from Uncle Burroughs) would travel off at right angles to the beeline and make a stand far out of sight from us. Eventually we would halloo our way together again, compare his different bearing on the hive with ours, and thus by triangulation find quite accurately our distance from the goal.

And so on a good day, as we closed in on our objective, the bees' flight was shortened, their working time and their number increased; and the bee boxes were alive with activity, the air noisy with traffic. At last came the exciting moment when, led into the very woods, we were so close to the tree itself that the flight was direct and decisive. Then the straining of bright eyes to discover just where, in some old hollow trunk, these canny insects were hoarding their golden treasure.

The story of this gentle sport should properly end here. We have had our delightful hike in the country, broken by long periods of rest, lolling in sunny fields. We have communed with Nature at her best—indeed, have spent the day in company with some of her most fascinating little creatures. We have had a good lunch. And we have found The Tree.

But, for the record, there is a sequel, at once distressing and delicious. If the tree is vulnerable, there comes by night an enlarged band of brigands, armed with lanterns, saws, axes, smoke guns, and wash boilers. After dark the bees are all at home, resting from a hard day's labor. Then is the safest time to plug all openings to their hive but one, and into that pour smoke till they are quiet. Now, before they wake, saw and chop away a great slab from the tree; expose huge, dripping stalactites of sweet, wild honeycomb; with sticky hands purloin this luscious prize and make off with the plunder in our wash boilers.

Let each judge for himself the morality of this midnight act of rapine. It takes, at least, hours of time, a woodsman's higher skill—but the fruit is delectable beyond description.

Such, as I recall, is the prose of hunting bees, brought back through conscious effort of the memory. Yet that which has an impulse of its own is the poetry of those delightful days, which comes to feeling, but not to words, spontaneously each year, as summer slants a little toward the fall and fields outcrop with nuggets of goldenrod.

END

Timing a bee's flight from bee box to honey tree and back again to gain a rough idea of the distance between these two points.

Oh, to Be Young Again and

Wesleyan Grove, Oak Bluffs, Martha's Vineyard, circa 1870.

CAMP MEETING

at Wesleyan Grove *by Howard G. Wilson*

It wasn't unusual for twelve to fifteen thousand persons to visit the Camp Grounds on a single Sunday in August!

Of the thousands of "summer people" who visit Martha's Vineyard each year, it is probable that many are unaware of a remarkable community known as the Camp Ground in Wesleyan Grove at Oak Bluffs. It is made up of more than 300 small ornate "gingerbread" cottages of tiny dimensions, each with a balcony over the front door and decorated with scroll work called "The American Carpenters' Renaissance." "This world-famed cottage area of the old Camp meeting ground is something out of another age." (*Vineyard Gazette*)

It began in a grove of venerable oak trees when seven fervent Methodists of Edgartown, Massachusetts, established a camp meeting site on a bluff overlooking Vineyard Sound. This was part and parcel of the revival movement and a forerunner of the camp ground of the future. As the years went by it grew, exerting conspicuous fascination for the thousands who came to worship as well as to have a good time.

Outdoor camp meeting services were said to have originated in Kentucky, *circa* 1800, and were a part of the religious revival of that period. This sunshine, blue-sky worship rapidly spread, first to the western states, then eastward. The preaching became more and more vehement. The parsons laid it on. Women wept. There was shouting, yelling, and singing that bordered on hysteria as lost souls came forward to be saved. Prayers and preaching usually began at the crack of dawn with fiery evangelistic spirit and frequently lasted well into the evening. Throughout the south and the west people heard about these camp meetings and came to see and to hear them, more out of curiosity than from any religious urge. But come they did, and many of them stayed.

Going to church out of doors had a revolutionary appeal. It was a relief from the sobriety

25

Above: *Bathing costumes varied widely even in the 19th century.* **Left:** *It would be hard to say which was the more decorated — the ladies or the cottages on "Rustic Avenue."* **Opposite:** *Even the horse is posing! Photography was a very popular hobby.*

of indoor Sunday services in severe and musty meeting houses. People liked the clean, cool fresh air, and in increasing numbers returned on Monday with tents to enjoy an ecclesiastical vacation on a Methodist salvation basis. So the Camp Meeting in America had its genesis.

Jeremiah Pease of Edgartown, Massachusetts, a lay exhorter with a reputation for piety, heard reports of these meetings and became inspired to spread the movement.

In the summer of 1835 this thin-lipped, straight-mouthed man with sharp, pointed nose arranged for the building of a rough shed made largely of old boards and driftwood, with a small platform for the preacher. In front of this improvised pulpit, an enclosed space was provided for the choir and for repentant sinners. In a semicircle facing the platform were nine tents occupied by different church groups. A canvas partition was discreetly strung through each tent; the women slept on one side, the men on the other; the visiting clergy slept in the shed. Everyone lay on clean straw spread on the ground. No cooking was done—the campers brought cold basket lunches, and life within the camp ground was carefree and intimate.

In those halcyon days there were no shower baths, no plumbing, no bathtubs, no available beds, and although there was hardly enough water to go around at the Camp Ground pump, the multitude of visitors had clean, sandy beaches and the salty Atlantic all around them.

Some of these thousands came to hear sermons by renowned preachers and to shout emotional amens as well as hallelujahs under the open sky. Most of them, however, came for the fun of it, as on any Sunday excursion.

This was the beginning of the Methodist Camp Meeting in Wesleyan Grove at Oak Bluffs.

Within a few years, in the mid 1860s, this Methodist Camp Meeting had become known throughout the world. At one time 15,000 persons braved the frequently rough crossing from Cape Cod to the Vineyard on High Sunday

during Camp Meeting Week in August. They came by steamer or sail from New Bedford, Providence, Falmouth and other far-flung points to take Vineyard Camp Ground life as they found it. On one Sunday the steamer *Cononicus* made not one but two round trips from Providence to the Eastville wharf, a landing more than a mile from the Camp Ground. Some people came over the sandy, narrow road in wagons, but most walked.

It had not occurred to Jeremiah Pease, the self-appointed camp meeting chorister and tent-master, to concern himself with the capacity of the arrangements and how many worshipers he could fit in. It would have been a premature question. Little did he realize that the outgrowth of this crude platform and less than a dozen tents was destined some years later to be visited by General U. S. Grant, then President of the United States, as well as Vice President Wilson, Secretary Robinson, Governor Talbot of Massachusetts and many other dignitaries of high rank and station.

The 50 years that followed the founding of Wesleyan Grove overshadowed any other in American history. The great war of 1861 to '65 had much to do with it. During these years the thinking and way of life of the nation underwent a revolution. The population more than tripled. Two thousand miles of railroad tracks grew to 100,000 miles. The telephone, telegraph, electric light and electric motor were invented. Gaslight, steamships, photography, as well as the luxury of central heating and indoor plumbing, came into general use. This indeed was the age of achievement. The transatlantic cable, the transcontinental railroad, the Brooklyn Bridge, public school systems, large corporations and mass production were accomplishments of an era of incredible achievement.

Despite this great scientific progress the Mid-Victorian Age became a symbol of propriety, prudishness and narrow-mindedness. The difference between the sexes was accentuated. The men were stern, bewhiskered and bald; the

Above: *The studied rusticity of the woven-branch benches contrasts oddly with the rococo cottages and formal clothing.* **Below,** *left: A sunny morning at "Mozart Cottage."* **Below,** *right: The piazzas of the closely built cottages seem to form a continuous concourse.*

Robert Perron photo

women, curvaceous, voluminously dressed with furbelows, hoop skirts and bustles. It has been said that architecture and clothing design are inseparable. The rococo buildings, over-decorated Mid-Victorian rooms crammed with over-stuffed furniture, ottomans, haircloth sofas, large gilt picture frames, waxed flowers under glass domes, and more and still more bric-a-brac were symbols and expressions of the way people lived and dressed.

In contrast, life at Wesleyan Grove was of necessity simple and informal. There were lots of young men and, report has it, many more beautiful young women. Introductions were unnecessary in those hallowed grounds; men, women, boys and girls met at the pump or at tent openings in various stages of dishabille and thought nothing of it. "Bluffing" (promenading on the bluff and bathing in the soft, warm Vineyard sea water) was part of the fun at Martha's Vineyard in those days. During the night many campers had only straw for a bed with the canopy of heaven for cover.

A night lamp was usually left burning in each of the tents, and the tent flaps remained open to the cool, salty breezes as well as to the tentmaster and watchman, who enjoyed his job so much he worked cheerfully without pay. He was privileged to look in to see what he could, but only in the line of duty.

Wesleyan Grove had grown to a camp of more than 50 tents; by 1851 there were upwards of a hundred. The Congregation on High Sunday during Camp Meeting Week numbered at that time more than 4,000 persons, with 50 or 60 ministers presiding over the exercises. The first, crude preacher's shed (the only one that had a roof) had been replaced by large church tents, each belonging to one of the mainland church groups. In some instances the church members lodged in these tents, and as there were no beds, they, too, slept on the ground. Private tents for families began to appear, which further stimulated the growth of Wesleyan Grove. These families enjoyed living by themselves, cooking by themselves, sleeping by themselves. They still belonged to the larger tent's company and continued to "enjoy the social means of grace with the mass of their brethren." Not everyone could have a family tent. One had to be vouched for by his pastor before receiving a license for a 20-foot camp site. The land remained the property of the Camp Meeting Association, as it does to this day.

By the memorable year of 1849, Wesleyan Grove was not so much a religious seat as it was a springboard towards making Martha's Vineyard a summer resort. Not only from the eastern states, but from the whole country, summer visitors came flocking to Wesleyan Grove.

"These thousands of people who frequent Martha's Vineyard at this season have more and fresher pleasures than those who summer at Newport or Longbranch," reported *Harper's Weekly*. "Here you see the latest fashions, and innocent flirtation is not unknown among the lads and lasses. They play croquet. Just below the steamboat landing there is a beach for bathing. And then there is fishing and sailing for those who are fond of aquatic sports, several good sailboats being always at anchor off the pier. When evening sets in, the girls put away their croquet and attend to the tea-making; then comes the evening service around the cottage doors, while outside the young people are promenading in the gaily lighted streets of the improvised village. Oh to be young again and at Wesleyan Grove when the skies were all clear, when the spirits leaped in expectancy and the sun and sea air touched the flesh with a caress which one could wish might last forever. Each generation chances upon its own fulfillment, and the generation which saw the end of the War between the States had no more characteristic fling into the realm of its desires than on the Camp Ground at Martha's Vineyard."

The Methodist Camp Meeting at the Vineyard continued to extend its enchantment. The number of family tents soon increased to 200 and made a complete circle around the larger Church Tents. Many were equipped with wooden floors and six-foot board sides which were left in place after the season had closed. This was the beginning of permanency and radically altered the substance of Wesleyan Grove.

The first complete cottage was built in 1859, and its extravagant and fantastic curvatures and ornamentations have persisted down through the years. The scroll work and lattice have been preserved, and this excellent scrimshaw fanciness is there today. These cottages are the best examples of Victorian scroll sawing and wood turning that remain in the United States; they have a small front veranda or stoop, double-arched church doors and, above, a still smaller balcony.

Wesleyan Grove, by now the most famous camp meeting in America, was getting somewhat out of hand religiously. The Elders of the Camp-Meeting Association clearly saw that either sanctity or frivolity was to prevail. Of the thousands who came to the Vineyard, not all were spiritually minded, nor were they attracted to Oak Bluffs by religious activities or spiritual aim. It was said by one clergyman that "the camp meetings might degenerate into a mammoth picnic." They already had!

There were still some who thought that "one of the great errors of late is making the recreation, rustification, and sociability of the occasion too great an object relatively."

In 1867, a group of farsighted Yankee businessmen recognized the monetary possibilities of Martha's Vineyard as a summer resort and formed the Oak Bluffs Land & Wharf Company, mindful of the fact that during the past decade it had not been uncommon for 12 to 15 thousand persons to visit Wesleyan Grove on a single Sunday in August.

The question arises how such an influx of humanity could get along for a day with so few essential conveniences and so little to live on. Many who came in the morning returned by boat in the evening. Those who stayed over slept either on boats or on the ever-present straw-covered ground under one of the Society Tents. The Camp-Meeting Association supplied drinking water from several wells, and licensed hawkers to shine shoes, rent towels and hold looking glasses for those who shaved. Other vendors sold coffee and sandwiches. The vicissitudes at Oak Bluffs made going there an experience.

The Oak Bluffs Land and Wharf Company observed that the thousands who came were not all prompted by religious zeal, and so acquired a large tract of land east of and contiguous to Wesleyan Grove. This acreage was laid out in medium-priced lots. A wharf was also built within easy walking distance from the Camp Ground and equally convenient to these building lots. It was freely admitted by those who managed the affairs of the Company that they were far more interested in profits than in prayers, although they never paid a dividend.

This real-estate boom on which many a quick profit was made became a mailed fist between the Camp-Meeting Association and the Oak Bluffs Land & Wharf Company. The folks in Wesleyan Grove decided to do something about it. In order to lock out sacrilege and lock in sanctity, the Association built a seven-foot fence surrounding its 36 acres. The large, wooden gates were shut tight and locked at 10:00 P.M. to separate the saintly from outside secular contamination. It is a matter of record, however, that many young blades—as well as some of the younger clergymen—admitted, years later, that there were places in that fence where the pickets were loose.

The Oak Bluffs Company soon realized that it was the better part of wisdom to cultivate Camp Ground goodwill and adopted a friendly and more liberal policy. The Company not only gave the Association free use of the new wharf but also deeded it a half acre of land to straighten out the boundary line between the two properties. Camp Ground management accepted with thanks, and to show its appreciation, immediately used the new acquisition for a colony of public outhouses!

This gift of land was never included in any prayers acknowledging divine favors.

In August 1870 the Church Tents gave way to a mammoth canvas covering of sailcloth. On the Sunday-evening opening of this canvas tabernacle seating 4,000 persons, a praise service was conducted by the chorister of Henry Ward Beecher's church in Brooklyn. A chorus of 500 voices sang "Come Ye Disconsolate." Nine years later this big top was taken down for the last time and replaced by the present Tabernacle of permanent steel construction.

At Oak Bluffs the Camp-Meeting Association is still active. The Mid-Victorian cottages, so close together they almost touch, circle the present Tabernacle, most of them on the original 20-foot plots. In fact, they are hardly separated at all and are more like a part of one large concourse.

This serious Cottager was apparently not one of those who would turn the Camp Meeting into one "mammoth picnic."

Years ago, at the season's end the campers formed a procession around the circle, singing a hymn and finally halting. Then each passed the other clasping hands and bidding their farewells with a "God be with you until we meet again."

Visitors to Martha's Vineyard can easily pass by Wesleyan Grove and not find it, although this quaint little settlement with its narrow, winding roads is as fascinating as it ever was. The cottagers own their buildings but do not own the land, which is leased to them. The Martha's Vineyard Camp-Meeting Association continues to maintain the grounds and watches over the cottages the year round, as it always has.

The original unique charter of the Association is preserved and is still carried on by the Association's board of directors.

One Wednesday in August is picked for "The Grand Illumination." This particular evening is the crowning event of the Camp Meeting season, as it has been for nearly a century. The grounds surrounding the tabernacle, known as Trinity Park, are aflame with Japanese lanterns hung on wires. Each cottager competes with his neighbor for the most brilliant display.

Another Camp Meeting feature on each Wednesday evening is the Community Sing sponsored by the Association. Thousands go to sing lustily the familiar old songs, and at the close to shake the hand of the person on either side.

Jeremiah Pease and his driftwood preacher's pulpit have long since gone the way of all things. The big top, the Church Society and family tents have been folded. The campground at Wesleyan Grove, with its scrimshaw cottages surrounding the tabernacle and its huge glistening cross, remains much the same as at the time of President Grant's visit in 1874. And each season the Camp Meeting folks or their descendants still return to their high peaked roofs, balconies and scroll work with the feeling of fellowship that binds these people together in a communion of religious thought and understanding. The present 300 campground cottages vividly reflect the Mid-Victorian era and symbolize permanence in the midst of change, due to the lasting power of goodness.

END

Elephants, camels, chariots, horses, horses, horses, calliope and bandwagon! Barnum & Bailey's circus comes to town — Bridgeport, Connecticut this page and New Haven town on the opposite page.

Courtesy L. F. Willard

CIRCUS PARADE

Here Come the Elephants
by Floyd Lee Bell

New Haven Colony Historical Society, courtesy T. S. Bronson

How many recall the days of the old Circus Parade? That glorious period when Circus-Coming-to-Town meant a day of jollity equal to, or perhaps surpassing, that of the Fourth of July?

Those of us born along the turn of the century remember well that cry, "Look out. The elephants are coming—watch your horses." There was the Gay Calliope—and the showman who pronounced it "cal-lie-o-pee" was promptly branded as a Johnny-Come-Lately—for it was always cally-ope. There were pretty girls in even prettier costumes astride gaily decked steeds—and what horses those were! There were cages of wild animals, or so one supposed, for the majority of these were carefully closed with perhaps just one or two cages of monkeys or a stalking tiger left open to whet the appetite. And at the middle of the Big Parade came the Great Band Wagon with 40 musicians perched high on its slanting top.

Of course, much earlier in the morning all of us had been down to the railroad yards to watch the Circus move into town. The Big Show moved in on four great trains, first the side shows and the menagerie train, and last the splendidly equipped passenger train bearing the performers. The Pullmans of those trains were almost permanent living quarters for them, particularly for the stars.

In those days, there were such circuses travelling through New England as Ringling Brothers, later to take over also the Barnum and Bailey Shows; Sells Floto; John G. Robinson, favorite of the Southland; Hagenbeck-Wallace; Gentry Brothers; King Brothers; Charles Sparks Circus; Yankee Robinson; Hunt Brothers (which still travels through New England each year by motor coach—today there are no railroad shows, meaning no circus is transported by rail.) There was Lemen Brothers, and a dozen more whose names now are just memories with some old-timers. But each show, regardless of size, had its parade down the main streets. The size of a circus was measured with the yardstick of "how many elephants does it have?" Some of the smaller ones with their two or three "ponderous pachyderms" were openly sneered at; but the true circus fan never missed visiting these shows as well as the big ones, for a circus was a circus and sawdust was sawdust no matter whether it showed at Prides Crossing or in Boston, Manchester, Portland, Hartford or Providence.

END

Diary of a Real Schoolteacher

by Amy G. Jarvis

"Five teachers in five years, and they ran the
last one out bodily... Them kids
need ploughin' under. Think ye can do it?"

FOREWORD: At the tender age of 19, and with a good deal of anxiety, the author left her native Boston for the tiny town of Hancock, Massachusetts, to assume her first teaching position. It was 1912, a time when running a small country school and living in a sparsely settled village in the Berkshire Hills was a continuing adventure. Passages taken from her diary are reproduced herewith exactly as she wrote them —except that the names have been changed (for obvious reasons!).

SUNDAY EVENING—SEPT. 1912. If my roommate's sister had not visited us that last weekend at Normal School, I would not be way out here in this country town of Hancock two hundred miles from home, about to start my first teaching in District School No. 2 where Faye taught last year and where she had such a wonderful time. Right now it does not look like that to me; it is all so strange that I seem to be in a different world where people speak a language that I do not understand. When I think of opening that school tomorrow morning, I have a dreadful feeling and wish I were right back in Boston. But here I am, and there is nothing I can do about it.

The long train ride to Pittsfield was interesting through lovely hills and valleys. Mr. Jones, the driver of the stage for Hancock, met me at the train. He is a short, fat man, weatherbeaten and very quiet. His eyes are bright blue and he spied me at once: "Guess ye'll be the new schoolma'am"—and held out a leathery hand. "I'll go git yer trunk." After it was strapped on the stage, he asked if I would ride "in" or "out" and I said "out," which meant "up" as well, for he hoisted me up over wheels, shafts, and onto a seat beside himself. Well, I thought, here I am for keeps; I will surely see the country.

We started with much straining, creaking, flourishings of the whip, and a few words for the horses' ears alone. Although I was the only passenger, he was not inclined to conversation, being very busy with his large chew of tobacco and the consequent spitting. So we jolted along, stopping now and then for him to deliver packages and newspapers to people along the route. He is the errand boy and takes his time visiting with each one. No doubt he told

ONE-ROOM SCHOOLHOUSE

Portrait of the author, 1912.

them who his passenger was and where she was going to teach. When we started going through the hills it was nearly dark and quite cold, so he wrapped me in a pungent horse blanket which kept me warm. The houses were miles apart and no lights except those shining faintly from the windows. We met few travelers and it was very still.

After a long, long time we drove into a yard and my companion said, "Here ye be, Miss." I tried to move and found I was so stiff that I had to fall off into his arms. Noticing that he did not unstrap my trunk, I asked if this were my boarding place, and he said, "No, Mr. White wanted I should bring ye here to supper first. He's head of the school board." At once I was nervous knowing I would be up for inspection and wondered what he would ask me. So I stumbled after Mr. Jones through a dark wood-shed and into a kitchen where a large man, dressed in an undershirt and overalls, sat at the head of a table and five or six children were waiting for supper upon the arrival of the schoolma'am.

"Wa'al," he said, rising to shake my hand limply, "here ye be at last. Set right down and eat, both o' ye." So we sat as we were, minus hats and coats—no washing of hands—to a supper of boiled beans, baking powder biscuits, apple pie, and boiled tea with half-milk. Mrs. White, busy at the stove, just smiled and kept filling our plates until we said, "No more, please." We all ate in deep silence until one child piped, "I seen yore picture." I had been asked to send a recent photograph with my application, and they were checking on me. Mr. White then spoke of my new position. "We've had awful bad luck with that school up thar. Five teachers in five years, and they ran the last one out bodily. [Poor Faye, she never told me that one!] I had to go and git her back. Them kids need ploughin' under. Think ye can do it?" He looked at me skeptically, so I said timidly, "I can try anyway."

By this time I was in no condition to answer any more questions, after riding for hours on a lumbering stage, and gave Mrs. White a desperate look—which she got at once. She hopped up, lighted a lantern, and I followed her out through a long shed to a "four-holer."

35

Then she scurried back into the kitchen. At least it was under cover, but what a long walk!

When I came back, Mr. White had a doubtful look, and the children still stared; but now I felt better able to cope with the situation and gave them what I hoped was a confident smile. He still wasn't sure of me but did wish me good luck, and Mrs. White smiled again.

So we started out again, driving only eight miles this time, once more arriving at a back door, going through another woodshed in the dark, and crawling up some back stairs, and knocking on another kitchen door. Mr. Jones seems to know his way around—probably from escorting the last five teachers along the same route. This time I received a real welcome from my landlady, Mrs. Larkin. Mr. Jones and a man downstairs brought up my trunk—and I was settled at last. The kitchen was warm and homelike with a lovely smell of cocoa, which she was keeping hot for me. She is the motherly type—fat and jolly with snapping black eyes and an ingrowing mouth, never having had her upper plate. But, bless her, she will board me and do my washing for two dollars a week! I liked her at once.

After drinking her good, hot cocoa and answering a few questions about my trip, she said I must be tired and showed me to a nice, large room with a comfortable bed, straw matting on the floor and braided rugs scattered around and a huge dresser and washstand, fully equipped. We said "good night" and I tumbled in, not even using the pink soap nor the embroidered towels. I slept ten solid hours. This morning I felt better, and after a breakfast of oatmeal, cream, boiled eggs, and cocoa steeped from the shells, I unpacked my trunk, thinking as I did so that I would not be wearing some of the things I had brought. After this I went over to the school, which is down the road a little way. I have never seen a school like it. It is a small, white building with one classroom and an entry for coats, with a shelf for dinner pails. There is a woodshed outside in which there is a toilet, deeply scarred with lewd drawings and printed names.

In the classroom there are white muslin sash curtains at the windows, three rows of double desks with two long benches in front for recitation, a wood stove in the middle of the room, my desk and chair at the right, and a closet for supplies at the left. There are blackboards on the left wall and a large clock. Out in the entry is a new water pail, dipper, and a pump. Over the desks and seats is a coat of varnish, recently applied, which will be sticky tomorrow. Mrs. Larkin's nephew, who lives downstairs, is the

Eighteen pupils in nine grades, ages 5-15; most walk three or more miles to school...

In this undocumented photo, teacher's elaborate hat looks out of place in the pastoral setting. She holds a "Textbook of Art Education".

janitor. I shall come home for my dinner at noon—and what will they do when I am gone?

MONDAY EVENING—SEPT. Well, I started "ploughin' under" to-day, and after one panicky moment when I forgot a line of the Lord's Prayer in the devotionals (I looked up to see if they noticed and they all had), things went along all right. There are eighteen pupils in nine grades, ages five to fifteen. Most of them walk three or more miles to school and bring their lunches in tin pails. The older boys leave school every spring to help on the farms, so they are often fifteen or sixteen when they finish the ninth grade. They gave me great cooperation today, getting out books, paper, pencils, and helping to fill in the register. I noticed they slipped out rather often for a drink of water and the resulting trip to the W. C. Some of the books are outmoded but some are like we have in Boston.

At recess they do not play, rather they stand in groups whispering to each other or pushing each other around. One of the boys kept peeking in the door and giggling in a silly way. Maybe their new shoes are uncomfortable after going barefoot all summer, or they may be mapping out a plan against the new teacher.

The schedule is a merry-go-round of classes for nine grades between the hours of nine and four, with half an hour for recess. I take one hour for my dinner at noon, while they eat their lunch. When I came back today they were all outside having a water fight and nearly all the girls were soaked. Of course, there was nothing to do but spend a while outdoors drying off, which is what they wanted.

THURSDAY EVENING—SEPT. I have had company. On Tuesday evening at nine-thirty, just as I was going to bed, Mrs. L. tapped on my door saying, "A young man to see you, Miss Brown." Dear me, at this time of night, I thought! I was tired but said I would be right out. In the kitchen was Roy Whitman, who had driven fifteen miles after doing his chores to look the new teacher over, and not at all concerned about the late hour. He is nice looking, tall, with that florid complexion they all have around here, reddish hair, beautiful white teeth—all of which makes him attractive. After talking a few minutes, he suggested taking a ride and off we went. His horse was tired, so we drove slowly while he did most of the talking about his farm, his family, and some gossip about the townspeople. He likes music, plays the violin, and asked me to join the choir, quite delighted that I sing alto for they have only one. The rehearsals are on Friday evening at the village church and he will call for me at nine o'clock. We got home at midnight. It must have been very late when he arrived at his farm in York state. I sure hated to get up this morning and the children gave me wise looks.

On Wednesday evening came Charles Horton, driving a mule named "Romeo," hitched to a brand new buggy. Charlie has a florid complexion also, but has badly fitting false teeth and wears a celluloid collar, very high and very stiff. He is pleasant but looks careworn. We, too, went for a drive behind Romeo, who has a wicked eye. He has a mate named Juliet, who is not to be trusted but Charlie drives her just the same.

He, too, asked me for choir rehearsal and was quite piqued when I told him that Roy had asked me; so he said, "How about church on Sunday?" I hadn't thought of that, but of course I would be dependent upon someone to take me, so I said "Yes, of course." He then said that we would go over to his sister's for dinner after church. She keeps house for his father, who lives in the village. Well, it seems that the boys in this town do most of their courting in a buggy, riding behind a horse or a mule.

SATURDAY EVENING—SEPT. Last night I went to choir rehearsal with Roy, and it was fun. We are seven—three sopranos, two altos, one bass, and one tenor. The organist is also the director and keeps time by nodding her head. They all love to sing and do it loudly, drowning me out completely. After an hour of this strenuous effort, they are all hungry so they have a lunch of cake and coffee. They are all friendly and have a good time. On the way home Charlie passed us, driving very fast. Maybe Romeo was skittish!

Mrs. Larkin waited up for me. She likes to hear the news, so we sat down together and had a little chat. I have a feeling that she doesn't like Roy very much, but she seemed delighted that I was going to church with Charlie tomorrow. I think she is a matchmaker and would very much like to see Charlie married, for she said he really does need a wife, and it seems that girls are scarce around here. I made no comment and am not thinking about getting married to anyone out here. I cannot imagine living here all the time; it is too desolate.

Charlie appeared with Romeo and his new buggy at ten o'clock this morning to take me to church. Everything was shining, including Charlie's face, and we rode away in style. When we arrived, I waited while he stabled Romeo. Then we went up in the choir loft and watched the people come in. The women sit fairly well front but the men, instead of sitting with their families, sit in the back pews and do not come forward until the last minute. They wear black suits. The women wear dark skirts and white shirtwaists with hats of a bygone day. The older children come, too, and sit very quietly with their mothers.

The service seemed very long to me with four hymns, all the verses, a soprano solo, anthem, and a good substantial sermon. After it was over, they shook hands with me very formally, and the minister invited me to his Sunday school class; he asked if I would take a class of boys who are hard to manage. Also, would I like to lead the service next Sunday evening? Dear me, I didn't realize the teacher was supposed to do all this church work. This needs thinking over.

MONDAY EVENING—SEPT. Did I say I wished the superintendent would come? Well, he did today and was I upset. I'm sure the children don't like him at all and there must be a reason. I told him some of the things we would need, and he just smiled and said, "We'll see what we can do," and then walked over to the blackboard and made a good drawing of cornstalks and pumpkins in a field. All the while the pupils were watching for something—which we soon found out. He had left his hat in the entry, and when he went to get it he found it full of water. He was very angry and came back with battle in his eye, but no one knew anything about it. He gave me a lecture on discipline; but I wasn't too badly upset for he did not impress me favorably and I hope he doesn't come too often.

THURSDAY—OCT. When I arrived at school this morning, I was startled to find four guns standing in the coat room. On inquiry, I found out that the older boys make a business of trapping and "skunking" and hunting. They have traps set all about in the woods, and they get two

The boys in this town do most of their courting in a buggy, riding behind a horse or mule.

Courtesy Elliott Allison

Also a small white building with one teacher and 18 students, this is the Dublin (N.H.) schoolhouse in December, 1892.

Strange the teacher didn't drop the switch for the photograph! Probably Portsmouth, New Hampshire, circa 1890.

Courtesy Strawbery Banke, Inc., Patch Collection

dollars for a good black skunk pelt—a week's board. I asked if they had permission to bring the guns to school, and they just looked at me as if I were crazy. They just said they had always done it. They go hunting at noon for they have no time in the morning and it gets dark so early. They must have been successful today, as we studied this afternoon in a strong odor. Whether I should report this to the school committee or not is a doubt in my mind since I imagine they are a law unto themselves about this. One of the boys in question is a son of a member of the board. However, I asked them not to bring the guns into the building again. Now we'll see what happens.

We are getting along with our work, after a fashion, but it doesn't satisfy me. There are so many periods that it all becomes routine with no time to work out new ideas. I'm going to combine a few classes next week and see how it goes. I would like more time for discussion. The seat work is all right. Jeremiah, in the first grade, is color blind and he always puts his green and orange pegs together. They whisper a lot but so far have not really disobeyed. I'm still the "new broom" of course. Pete reported that someone had eaten his lunch—the pail was there empty—so I made everyone give him something and he had more than usual, the others less. It may not happen again. Pete's mother is the cook for a rich man who spends his summers in the Berkshires not far from here, and she can probably cook a little better than their mothers.

MONDAY EVENING—Oct. The folks downstairs had a husking bee Saturday night and what fun we had! The people came from miles around to help husk the corn which was piled on the barn floor. Lanterns were hung on pegs and gave a weird light. We sat around on the floor husking and throwing the husks into another pile. There were plenty of red ears, and when a young man gets one and starts for you, you're supposed to run anywhere out of sight for they are bashful about kissing in public. I began to suspect they found the same red ears over and over. I'm sure there couldn't be that many in the whole cornfield. We were sneezing continually for the dust was terrible.

A husking bee Saturday night and what fun we had! We danced the Money Musk, quadrilles, Portland Fancy and Virginia Reel...

After it was all done, they cleared the floor for dancing. Old Percy came with his fiddle, and somebody brought a mouth organ, and it began. We danced the Money Musk, quadrilles, Portland Fancy, and Virginia Reel to Percy's calling, "Sashay forward and back," "Swing her round and round," "Bow to your partner," "The other way," "All march," etc., until I was dizzy and very hot. When they swing you, you nearly hit the rafters, coming down only to go up again with another partner. They try to outdo each other! Between times, we drank quantities of cider and once in a while I smelled something stronger.

SUNDAY EVENING—OCT. Well, diary, what would I do without you? I tell you all my troubles, joys, and secrets, and you are so receptive. I usually have a nightly talk with Mrs. Larkin, who is like a mother to me, and often gives me sound advice and helps me over the rough places. Roy drove me to church this morning and invited me to have dinner with his cousin Elsa, who is the church organist. Charlie didn't take this very well, but I feel I have a right to go where I please and with whom and no questions asked, and besides Roy asked me last week. So after Sunday school, for I have that class of boys who are indeed hard to manage, we drove to the other side of town, following Elsa and her father, who is a widower.

They have a fine farm with a nice big, white house on a hill from which there is a grand view. Elsa has a hired girl so has less to do than many of the women. After a good dinner, Elsa and I played duets, then Roy played his violin (which I thought was terrible), and we all sang hymns. Elsa received her musical training in Boston. Her father and Roy have both been there so they feel they have been around. Roy feels that I should have more in common with them than I ever could have with Charlie, who has only been as far as Pittsfield. I'm not so sure about that, but I do know that I'm not serious about either of them. Of course, I realize that there is a scarcity of girls in this town and the young men have rather a hard time of it.

I met another young man at church today. His name is Guy Montez and he lives in the village. I discovered that his sister was in my class in Normal School, so we felt acquainted at once. He asked me to the Grange dance on Wednesday evening in Ashton, seven miles away, and I am going. I love to dance and neither Charlie nor Roy know how. Guy lives with his grandmother, as he has neither father nor mother, and he works in the mill.

FRIDAY EVENING—NOV. I was too tired to write last night, so here goes tonight. I went to the dance Wednesday with Guy and had a wonderful time. He came at eight o'clock, not having any chores to do, looking very nice in his fur coat and hat. I wore my green silk with black velvet girdle. Mrs. Larkin was sure I would freeze to death if I didn't wear a pair of woolen leggings which she helped me work into. I really wasn't cold at all. I had a fur coat and Guy had a foot warmer, which is sort of a square metal box with hot coals inside, in the sleigh and it was all very cozy. We arrived at Ashton about nine o'clock, just in time. The fiddlers were warming up, and there was an organ and a drum, the first fiddler being the caller. The hall was large, well lighted with oil lamps, a row of settees on three sides of the room, a huge stove in one corner, and the orchestra on a platform in the opposite corner.

"Take your partners for the quadrille," the fiddler called, and we made up sets—eight in each. We started to Hull's Victory. Everybody does the square dances but only a few do the waltzes and two steps and the schottische, which I love to do in double-quick time. At intermission we had sandwiches and coffee downstairs at long tables and everyone was very jolly. Guy is a wonderful dancer, and I enjoyed every minute of it.

At two o'clock we left for the seven-mile drive home and found a lot to talk about. Guy says he has a steady girl—a teacher in the village who is back for the second year—but she doesn't dance and doesn't mind if he takes out another girl once in a while. I wonder about that! Mrs.

Larkin left some cocoa on the back of the stove. She thinks of everything.

WEDNESDAY—NOV. Tomorrow is Thanksgiving Day—my first away from home. I am going to eat dinner with Charlie and his family in the village and stay all night this time. Mrs. Larkin invited me to eat with her but I feel her family will have a better time by themselves.

ON THE TRAIN TO BOSTON—SATURDAY—DEC. The snow-covered hills are receding gradually as I get nearer to Boston. It seems almost as strange to be going home as it did when I came here four months ago. Mrs. Larkin was almost in tears this morning, as indeed was Charlie. He put me on the train, put my luggage around me, dropped his gift in my lap—a box of candy—kissed me quickly, and said "Good-bye, Amy, I'll count the days until you come back." Right now he seems far away in a different world where the people live simply, working hard for so little, yet seem to be happy and contented with no desire to live elsewhere. I have gained ten pounds and never felt so well in my life. The air now has changed to that city smell.

ON THE TRAIN TO PITTSFIELD—SUN. JAN. 1913. My two weeks' vacation has gone so quickly. Soon we shall be in Pittsfield where Charlie will meet me and we will have a long sleigh ride through the hills to Hancock. He wrote that he had been lonesome and was looking forward to my return. Roy also wrote and said that we must see more of each other from now on, that the Grange is going to give a play in January,

Interior of the Alburgh (Vt.) stone schoolhouse, September, 1899. Another fancy hat.

Even the children sensed something was wrong — the old fox!

"District School," and they have a part for me. Both Charlie and Roy will be in it, and there will be the same old question: "Who will take me when?" Charlie has to go by our house to get anywhere, and Roy has to drive twenty miles from the other side of town from York state, so Charlie has the advantage. If he weren't so serious I would like it better. My conscience troubles me a little, but not with Roy. Things do not go so deep with him. The townsfolk recommend Charlie—a good steady fellow though he seems to have hard luck. I really have more fun with Roy and nothing to worry me.

MONDAY EVENING—JAN. Being a country schoolma'am has its compensations. Never were any pupils happier than mine when they saw me again—so eager to tell me everything that had happened in two weeks. Robert, the oldest boy, is now sixteen and a head taller than I am. Sometimes when I catch him looking at me, how he blushes! Charlie was very glad to see me. He kissed me twice and said it was a long vacation. He had a little hard luck this time—his horse was sick, one cow died, and he, himself, had a very bad cold. He really does need a wife, but not one like me, even though he may think so.

When I came to school this morning, I found a coiled spring in my chair waiting for me to sit on it. I put it on my desk where they could all see it and left it there all day. Except for a spell of giggling it really fell flat. I didn't even ask who put it there.

FRIDAY EVENING—FEB. Tonight I went with Charlie to my first prayer meeting. On the way home Charlie was quite serious and drove Juliet slowly. He gave me some unasked-for advice about going places with Roy, says he is a ladies' man and would never be true to me. I said I hadn't thought of his being true or not, but I liked him and if I wanted to go anywhere with him I would, and didn't consider it anyone's business. I can see how Charlie's mind is running. I'll have to change its course somehow. There are so few girls in this town that the men are getting desperate. I haven't any idea of getting married for a long time yet. And I don't like rushing.

TUESDAY AFTERNOON—FEB. It is now half past four and still nice and warm in the schoolroom. Today I had a new experience, and I am a little nervous about it. The superintendent was here this afternoon and spoke about a teachers' meeting to be held in Pittsfield next week. He has arranged for Mr. Estes to drive us three teachers in his double sleigh for fifty cents. Mr. Franklin will also drive. But that isn't what is bothering me. At recess he sent all the children out of doors and wrote a note which he held up for me to see. It read thus: "How would you like to exchange your fifty cents for a kiss?" Then he tore it into tiny bits and threw them into the stove. I just stood there saying nothing and wanting to get out-of-doors. Finally, I said, "No, no," and reached for the bell and called the children in five minutes early. Then he smiled in a funny way and walked around the room pretending to look at the children's work. Even the children sensed something was wrong. I could tell by their expressions. What shall I do? I want to keep my job, but if he is like that, I can't stand it. I think I will tell Mrs. Larkin—she will know what to do. He must be at least fifty years old, and he is married and has children. The old fox!

WEDNESDAY EVENING—FEB. Well, I feel better now. I am so glad I told Mrs. Larkin my trouble. The Chairman of the School Board is her brother-in-law, and she says he will fix this "would-be Romeo." I'm to let her know if anything happens again. It seems that his reputation is none too good and, though he has been here three years, it doesn't mean that he can stay forever. I feel so relieved. Now I can go to the convention and enjoy it. I imagine I will hear many plans, ideas, and theories which are not applicable to this district, however.

THURSDAY AFTERNOON—FEB. The play is over, and what a crowd we had! There was just one scene—the country schoolroom with double desks—and we were all dressed as children, with pigtails, hair ribbons, short socks, etc. Roy and I got a big hand for our song "Reuben

I keep seeing a little white schoolhouse and a mule with one ear up and one down.

and Rachel." Some of the jokes were quite personal. This is what one pupil recited: "Roy and Charlie are sweet on teacher/I wonder which one will get to the preacher." They all shouted their appreciation of that one. We all sang "School Days" as a finale.

Roy drove me home last night. He, too, is beginning to get serious. He thinks we are "just made for each other"—interested in the same things—and we could have wonderful times together if only I wouldn't go with anyone else. Now just think of that!

Well, supper is ready. The days are longer now and spring is on the way. The sap will soon be running and that means sugaring time and tapping the trees. The people downstairs have a great many sugar maples and do quite a business every spring.

Next Saturday I shall go home for a two weeks' vacation. Last night, while driving home from church, Charlie asked what my favorite color was and seemed quite surprised when I said "Red." He is having his house fixed up with the idea of getting married I feel sure. I hope he doesn't pop the question, for I shall say "No" and there will be no more rides for me. While I am on vacation the school board will install the equipment for the classes in cooking and manual training. This is going to be somewhat of an experiment and a joke to the parents. I shall bring back my first lessons in domestic science and try them out.

SUNDAY AFTERNOON—MARCH. At last I am on my way home once more. Charlie took me to the train and was unusually nice; but he did not propose—not yet. Maybe he could not find any red wallpaper. To tell the truth, I think he's afraid I'll say "No." I really do like him though. Now we are leaving the snow country and things are looking a bit like spring. I shall know this time whether or not I will get a new position I want at home.

SATURDAY AFTERNOON—APRIL. Back again in Hancock after a vacation at home and, best of all, I am to have that new position—third and fourth grades in Brockton. Charlie met me in Pittsfield. How his face does light up when he sees me! Even his dapple-gray horse neighed in welcome. It is good to be back and breathe this wonderful air again. There is still snow on the hills. We are ready to start classes in domestic science and manual training. Tomorrow is Sunday, with two services at church and dinner at May's in between. Also that class of boys in Sunday school. Roy has invited me to spend the next weekend with his cousin Elsie. He will be there and is planning a good time for two days. Mrs. Larkin doesn't approve but doesn't dare say anything except, "It's no feather in your cap to go there."

It is warmer—the air has a smell of spring and, best of all, the mud is drying up. Wagon wheels up to the hubs in mud and muddy boots scraping the schoolroom floor will soon be a thing of the past.

SUNDAY EVENING—MAY—TWO WEEKS LATER. Friday night Mrs. Larkin's daughter, Lucy, and I started for a revival meeting in the next town. As we came around the corner by the school, instead of a narrow white outbuilding, there were four black holes staring at us. Lucy gave one whoop and said, "They've done it again!" It seems that once a year toward the end of the term, some few naughty boys tip over the W. C. and then the school board has to get a team and pull it back. So back we went to tell Mrs. Larkin's son, John. Considerate of them to wait until Friday anyway!

Off we went again. Reaching the church a little late, we sat in a back pew. Every little while when we thought of the outbuilding we were seized with a fit of laughter. This seemed to annoy the preacher, who may have thought we were being flippant, for soon an usher came down the aisles asking people to go up front "if they wanted to feel the power of God." He stopped by us, so we went up singing "Rescue the Perishing" with all our hearts, as it seemed to stop the giggles. We should have told him why we were laughing.

Well, school will close in two weeks and I

Snapshot of the author riding with "Charlie" behind his dapple-gray the winter of 1912-1913 in Hancock, Massachusetts.

have told the children I am not coming back. How sad they all looked! They wanted to say something but didn't know what. They hung around my desk after school, giving me invitations to supper, etc. A teacher in a country school gets close to her pupils and learns how to control them by affection and kindness. She is alone, with no one to consult in a bad situation, and she has to be somewhat of a diplomat and to know human nature.

SATURDAY EVENING—JUNE. I have told Charlie that I am not coming back and he cannot talk about it. Mrs. Larkin says she will miss me like a daughter, and the superintendent offered me fifteen dollars a week if I would stay.

ON THE TRAIN—PITTSFIELD TO BOSTON. School is now over, and I do feel sad about it all. The children stood in line for a good-bye kiss, boys as well as girls. Next year I am to teach in a city school, forty pupils in one room, and a principal in the building to carry the responsibility; but I will never have the close, friendly feeling that this little district school has given me; it has been a rewarding experience I shall never forget. Mrs. Larkin gave me a beautiful sweater which I thought she was making for her daughter, and we both cried over it. She has been wonderful to me. Roy drove into the yard just as Charlie and I were starting for the train. He came to say "Good-bye," gave me a picture of himself, and said he was coming to Boston to see me. I shall miss him, too, for he was always gay and full of fun.

Now I come to the last evening when Charlie and I went to ride. It was a perfectly gorgeous night—full moon and warm for this time of year. He drove slowly, and we were both uncomfortable—each for a different reason. He started talking about his house, his farm, how well he had done this year, and his next year's plans. Finally he asked me if I would "have him." I was not to think he wanted his answer at once, but he would like some encouragement —which I could not give. He was terribly disappointed, and I felt conscience-stricken as I probably have encouraged him more or less and he is serious minded. We drove home, almost in silence until we were nearly there. Then he said he would take me to the train and, if I felt any different in the morning, I could tell him, which of course I didn't. As I think how he looked and how he must have felt I do indeed feel sorry, but it was the only possible thing for both of us. I am not the kind of woman he needs. I only hope he will not think too badly of me and will find some nice girl who will make him happy.

We are nearing Boston with its city smells and crowds of people. I find it hard to take; I keep seeing a little white schoolhouse and a mule with one ear up and one down.   END

Canoeing on the Charles

Few rivers in the country saw as many canoes as did the Charles....

For about twenty fabulous years, 1900 to 1920, canoeing on the Charles River in Massachusetts as a sport and favorite pastime was big business. Thousands of canoes were afloat on the water during pleasant Saturdays, Sundays, and holidays. There was much listening to band concerts, watching of fireworks, staying out all night on the river.

During this heyday afloat, few if any rivers in the country saw as many canoes as did the Charles, (once lovingly known as Quinobequin by the resident Algonquin Indians). Canoe houses in this busy, carefree period (just before the homely, noisy automobile) dotted the river banks at Cambridge, Waltham, Riverside, Dedham and Natick.

In the old days, before the dams, it was possible to paddle 65½ miles by canoe all the way from Factory Pond, above West Medway, to the harbor in Boston. Time? About 20 hours. But that was the era before canoeing became a pleasure and a fashion on the lordly Charles. There is general agreement that what whetted interest in canoeing as a practical pastime was the introduction of exciting war canoe racing in the early 1900's. These annual races, plus completion of Norumbega as a fine park in the same general period, heightened interest in river sports. Along with the opening of the Park to the public went the erection of a boathouse there in 1898. As canoeing quickly gained in popularity, other boathouses sprung up until at last they fairly dotted the river, perhaps with heaviest concentration being in that picturesque area of bends-in-the-river which stretched from Riverside to Waltham.

Earl H. Ordway, who for many years coached the Lasell Junior College canoe club crew,

SUNDAY ON THE RIVER

by Arthur F. Joy

"... a pleasure and a fashion..."

Above: *A spirited water fight entertains watchers waiting to paddle their own canoes.* **Opposite:** *Raising their paddles, canoeists salute as the National Anthem is played during a Sunday band concert. July, 1919. Note morning glory horn in canoe right rear.* **Below:** *The Onawa Club on the Charles about 1915.*

Courtesy Waltham Historical Society

remembered a certain afternoon in the summer of 1903, "when I went down to the bridge at Riverside station. You simply could not see the river for canoes. There was a band concert going on and many hundreds of onlookers surrounded the area, reclining in their canoes, enjoying the open air and the festive music.

"How wonderful it was to take a trip in an open trolley from Boston, hire a canoe at Riverside for about 25¢ an hour, and paddle your best girl up and down the river."

An unusual custom was introduced in 1911. It involved the towing of a big scow by a motorboat on the river. On this scow two or three bands would be playing. A big piano was included. This happy event occurred every Saturday night. For quite some time thereafter anywhere from fifty to two hundred canoes would be hitched up behind the scow, following along, the canoeists happily listening or singing to the music.

Ordway was pilot of that motorboat. "Some of the leading boathouses and canoe organizations were behind this innovation, which, I should add, was quite popular while it lasted. We would tow this musical procession up and down the river, the bands playing, many of the canoeists singing along with the music as, by means of tow topes, they got a wonderful, relaxing free ride behind that scow."

Marathon canoe races—from Riverside to the Moody Street bridge, Waltham, and return—were very popular. The biggest day for this was Memorial Day. Two clubs in Waltham, as well as the Newton Boat Club, Robertson's and Young's boathouses were active backers of these races. These clubs would get together and promote the various meets. In the marathon

Girls from Lasell Seminary, Auburndale, Massachusetts, June, 1902. The canoe bow bears the monogram of the Lasell Canoe Club, formed 1894 — "LCC."

race, each man paddled all the way—about five miles. The winner became a local hero.

There were nine boathouses in Auburndale alone. Canoeing became so popular and the waters so crowded that accidents happened. The police fished out many a couple.

A retired Metropolitan Police Commission lieutenant, Daniel MacLeod, described the heyday of canoeing on the ever-popular Charles thus:

"I came on duty here May 15, 1902. Norumbega Park was in full bloom then. Those popular open electric cars of the Commonwealth Street Railway brought summertime pleasure-seekers by the thousands. Glad to be rid of the heat of the city, about one-third of this crowd headed for the Park and its amusements. The other two-thirds made for the river and canoes. Most of our work was rescue in the early days. Canoes tipped easily and the novice was usually a victim at one time or another."

The Patrol headquarters was prepared not only to pull canoeists out of the water, but also by means of special quick-drying equipment, to help them with their wet clothes.

"After they rinsed out their garments in the big bath tub, they hung them up in the drying room. In no time at all our gas heaters and fans would have their clothes dry and ready to wear—wrinkled, but wearable."

Lieutenant MacLeod remembered that buttered popcorn and cold soda sold the fastest along the river in those days. Refreshment stands were many.

"And for entertainment, portable phonographs, the ones with the morning glory horns, were very popular. Sometimes two or three mandolin or guitar players would tie their canoes together and play and sing as they floated, with their girls, downriver. It was a pretty sight. Folks who didn't hire canoes would line the bridge [Weston Bridge] and watch from above. It got to be known as 'rubber neck bridge.' The girls in the canoes would have little parasols to ward off the hot sun. Pretty girls would lie on fancy cushions as their beaus, kneeling on one knee, paddled leisurely along, chatting as they went. There was a lot of canoeing at night, of pulling up and anchoring by the riverbank to spoon under the protective netting. There were a lot of mosquitoes along the river in those days—before spraying with chemicals and before oil slicks from motorboats smothered the larvae."

MacLeod estimated that at one time there were over five thousand canoes owned and stored in the various boathouses between the Riverside Recreation Grounds and the Moody Street dam in Waltham.

"On Saturday nights," MacLeod reminisced, "the old Salem Cadet Band used to play for the crowds at Newton Boat Club. The river there would be so filled, so choked with canoes that I had to pull my way through, on

Double-ender patrol boat and Patrolman Harry Chaisson in front of the Norumbega boathouse in 1905.

patrol. Our boats were built for speed. They were good double end craft and you could paddle them along about as fast as a canoe. I remember one time on the river when I came upon two fellows floundering in the water. I pulled them out and realized they were drunk as fools. At the Station we dried them off and then, to their surprise, we locked them up. There was no particular law against renting a canoe to drinkers, but we frowned on it."

Along with drinking and staying out all night on the river, came some rowdyism. This, in turn, threatening the good trade as it did, ushered in the era of the constant river patrol. From then on, river police quelled fights, rescued tipovers, stopped drinking whenever they could.

"I remember," MacLeod continued, "one young man as he went toward his canoe. He weaved before he got to it and it was obvious that he had been drinking. I wanted to save him from a possible spill and I told the rookie officer with me at the time to get into his own boat, follow along, and stop the drunk. This officer, a new man with me, hurried to carry out my orders. He was so energetic about it that as he jumped into his boat it tipped and overboard he went. I took *him* to the Station instead of the drunk!"

On hot summer nights, many canoeists stayed out all night. The regulars would equip their canoes with a mosquito netting looped over the bows. Then, with portable phonographs, lots of comfortable cushions and a big carpet mat along the floor, they would spend a comfortable evening on the river. It might be hot in the city, but along the Charles there generally was a welcome breeze.

One "regular" explained, "We used citronella oil in those times for the mosquitoes. When you were paddling, you didn't notice the insects so much. We had rubberized blankets in case of showers, and there used to be band concerts until 2 A.M. On Fox Island there was a concert every week. Fireworks, too. I remember the old tube records, before the flat ones came in, and the portable phonographs with morning glory horns. Some of those big horns could broadcast a melody good and clear a mile down the river! Yes, and the mandolin clubs. Some of us used to take a lunch and stay up all night. It was great fun. After the automobile came in, canoeing like that went out fast."

So the hectic days of paddling-your-own-canoe are over. Now the river is filled with outboards, sailboats, excursion craft, cabin jobs —swift, loud speedboats of all shapes, sizes and colors. Gone is the quiet, the serene Sunday afternoon on the river when the only sound was the ripple of water as it swirled gently past the paddle; gone is the friendly group singing, the big band concert and the morning glory horn, the spectacular fireworks display. Gone is the day when canoeing was "the most." END

The Moxie Team
by Edna Hills Humphrey

Charles E. Hills photographed en route during his 1899 tour as the Moxie man.

"Moxie! Moxie!" Two small boys ran beside the Moxie team as it drew up at a Fitchburg, Massachusetts, drug store. The driver, nattily attired in uniform and matching cap, tied the horse to a hitching post and entered the store.

My father was the Moxie man, part of a Moxie team of 1899; some oldsters may remember the one-horse wagon with a seat for the driver and behind him a large replica of a Moxie

"NERVE FOOD"

One good reason why by 1915 Moxie was the most popular soft drink in New England

bottle bearing the legend, "Moxie Nerve Food—Delicious and Healthful—Feeds the Nerves."

Moxie is a soft drink made from herbs and sugar, still to be found in some areas of New England. Manufactured in Boston and New York, it was originally distributed west to the Mississippi and south to Florida. Moxie was invented in the early 1890s by Dr. Augustine Thompson of Lowell, Massachusetts—an era

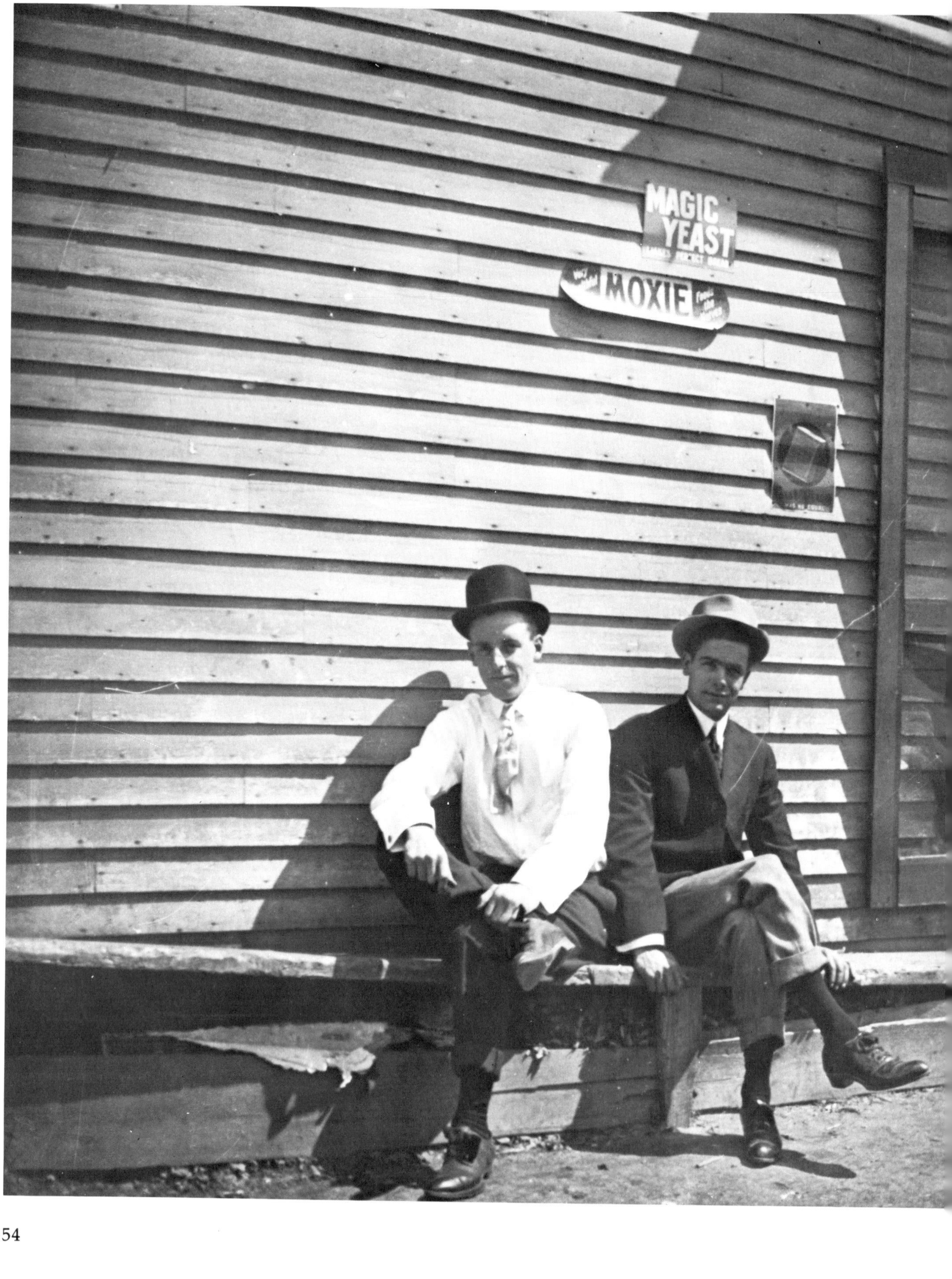
MAGIC
YEAST
MOXIE

when huge profits were made from the sale of patent medicines such as Hood's Sarsaparilla and Father John's Medicine. Dr. Thompson's concoction was known as Moxie Nerve Food until the patent medicine market declined, when it was sold simply as a carbonated soft drink —Moxie.

In order to help pay his way through medical school, my father, Charles E. Hills, spent his 1899 summer vacation from Dartmouth College as a Moxie man. The Moxie team was a unique way of distributing advertising material and keeping the name Moxie before southern New England. The large bottle on his wagon carried pictures of the Moxie bottle, sidewalk signs, small hanging signs, window stickers and tin signs with cherry frames for bicycle stands. The bottle also held Father's meagre wardrobe— and certainly some rain gear, since there was no top to the wagon.

On a typical day, Father would leave the hotel where he had spent the night (at an average rate of $2.50, including stabling and feed for the horse and his own supper and breakfast) at 8 A.M. and visit several towns, stopping at the last for the night. Miles traveled depended to a large extent on the condition of the roads. The roads were what Father called "very hard" (poor) on one trip that started in Hartford, Connecticut, and ended that night in Andover, only 18 miles away! His salary was $12.00 a week, plus room and board. At the end of the college vacation, the work of Dr. Charles E. Hills for the Moxie Nerve Food Company terminated, and he returned to Dartmouth. But he had gained valuable experience, become acquainted with much of southern New England, and helped to keep Moxie in the public eye.

This ingenious advertising campaign undoubtedly was one good reason why by 1915 Moxie was the most popular soft drink in New England; in 1931, its sales had achieved the then staggering total of eight million bottles yearly! Moreover, the name made a place for itself (without initial capital) in the English language dictionary as a slang term for pep, vigor, courage or nerve—"he's full of moxie." We presume that the word is of Indian origin. It exists as the name of the Moxie Falls in Maine, whose stream runs into the Kennebec.

END

The sign on the wall of this village store is evidence of a visit from the Moxie man. The large bottle on his wagon was filled with signs like this and other advertising material.

Down by the Depot

by Stephen S. Bean

Our village station was a small, once red, soot-stained building across from the shingled, roofed, wooden bridge leading over the Warner River to the Mink Hills. The front room was dingy and drab. Roger Gage, Station Agent and Postmaster, kept the windows clean, but the floor was dark and worn with stains from muddy boots over the years.

The pot-bellied, wood-burning stove stood in the center, its rusty pipe angling to the chimney at the far end. Heavy benches were nailed to two walls. Backed to a third wall were sparsely laden grocery display shelves. A glass case contained a few loose pounds of grayish chocolate; on the counter in front of the shelves were some dried-out packs of "Lon Bean's 3 for 5¢ Seegars".

RAILROAD STATIONS

The depot is gone, but there are those who remember when they heard the first, faint long *who-whoo-who-whoo* **clear down the track at Colbey's Crossing....**

Roger always told his customers candy and tobacco improved with age! On the fourth side, the Station Agent had his narrow office. There was a small rectangular window with metal bars through which he pushed tickets when any of Waterloo's 30 year-round, or 50 summer residents, or the farm folks from miles around went down to Warner or even to Concord for a day's shopping. On the walls were Boston and Maine Railway advertisements inviting excursions to such alluring places as Sunapee Lake and distant Hampton Beach.

Even more exciting were the posters vividly describing train robbers wanted "Dead or Alive." Many a farm lad or summer boy, waiting for the afternoon train to come returning

Depot at Livermore, New Hampshire, a busy logging town way back when, serviced by the P & C Railroad.

Top: *A busy morning at Ashuelot (N.H.) Station, 1859.* **Bottom left:** *"Good-bye, Grandpa." Back to school and the city after a summer on the farm. White River Junction, Vermont. 1895.* **Right:** *North Carver, Massachusetts. A double-barreled load.*

Courtesy H. E. Wiggin

58

empty milk cans and chicken crates, painstakingly read every word about these desperados and wished that he could capture one of them and receive the $500 fortune.

With as great amazement as greets today's hurtling through space, one heard the clattering telegraph on the table before the bay window overlooking the track. Peeking into the office wide-eyed, the boys and girls watched both the key and the agent. He would listen to the dots and dashes for a minute or two, then reach a forefinger forward and send messages up north to Bradford or down south to Contoocook. The baggage room occupied the building's rear. There was located the cracker barrel and an ice-box from the cool depths of which Roger would pull out quart-size bottles of home made root beer on the rare occasions when children or grown-ups had five cents to squander.

The little gray-red depots are nearly gone. In the early 1900s, however, village and country way stations were important. Lumber was hauled to them by yokes of oxen. Livestock, milk and cream, eggs, poultry, apples and other produce were shipped thence in the freight or baggage cars to merchants and middlemen in the city. On rainy days it was good news to a boy when father said, "Son, after you finish slopping the hogs, better hitch up Joe, go fetch the milk cans at the depot, and while you are there pick up two bushels of oats and a bag of middlings next door."

The arrival at Waterloo of the 4:30 up train from Concord, which may have picked up a passenger or two from the express leaving Boston at noon, was the occasion for a community gathering. It had two or, on Fridays and Saturdays in the summer, three passenger coaches as well as a mail and a baggage car. And around the Fourth of July there were two engines and a parlor car at the rear for the city folks going to spend the summer at their remodeled farmhouses in New London and Sunapee Lake. When the Pullman again appeared going south early in September, the farmers knew it was high time to harvest their last crops and pack straw well over the foundation tops of their houses.

Men and boys gathered at the station early. Their womenfolk came later. Finally at the dramatic hour, as "Number 57" appeared around the bend, Nehemiah G. Ordway, my "Uncle Miah," long-time former Territorial Governor of the Dakotas, he of the mysteriously acquired affluence, sanctimonious mien, and gigantic stature, would wheel into the yard in his Concord buggy hauled by the spanking Morgans "Bismarck" and "Fargo." As the summer progressed and the previous fall's cider became harder, his appearances became progressively more dashing and more impressive. Indeed the *Kearsarge Independent and Times* for August 30, 1908, reported, "We are sorry to learn that last Saturday Gov. Nehemiah G. Ordway upon entering the Waterloo Station precipitated through a glass case and suffered numerous cuts on his face, right arm and shoulder. However, it may be reported that after the Governor recovered from his original numbness and the first shock he regained his usual composure and as of this printing is resting as comfortably as could be expected."

Waterloo's other distinguished citizen was U.S. Senator William E. Chandler, my "Uncle William." Less resplendent and flamboyant than most Senators of that "Claghorn" period, he of sedate mien and dapper appearance, garbed in immaculate white ducks and Panama straw, never came down the hill to the station until precisely 15 minutes after the 4:30 had departed. Accompanied by his Administrative Assistant, he would appear at Roger's ticket window, the bars would be pushed up, and the priority-sorted senatorial mail came out in bales while we little people waited in awe at the enormity of Uncle William's correspondence. Little did any of us realize until decades later that 90 percent of the mail emanating from the heart of our Government in the Nation's Capitol quickly found its resting place in the waste basket!

The depot is gone, but there are those who remember when they heard the first, faint, long, *who-whoo-who-whoo* clear down the track at Colbey's Crossing. Farmers would pull silver watches on leather thongs from overall pockets and say, "Bill is five minutes late this afternoon, but he can make it up on the straight run through Melvins." Great fun was the game of putting one's ear to the rail and listening to see who first could detect the haunting, thin, high-pitched song of steel as the train came nearer. Then we would hear the far-away whistle and, in three or four minutes, old 57 would come around the bend. There was a clattering of metal, the wild clanging of the bell, the hiss of escaping steam as the train ground to a halt.

Greetings were called back and forth as the baggage man tossed jugs and crates onto the waiting carts. The engineer leaned from his cab and swapped greetings; the conductor watched while the unloading went on. Then he waved his arm to the engineer and shouted,

"Pick up the oats at Shackley's and watch the train come in."

"All aboard," whether any one was getting on or not. There was a series of short, loud, sharp, staccato blasts as the engineer opened the throttle. The wheels took hold, the bell clanged, and the train started toward the next station.

As a farmer's boy drove home and heard the lonesome-sounding whistle far up the line toward Burnt Hill he made a promise to himself: some day he would be on that train, riding away to life's high adventure—even perhaps to the Halls of Congress or a distant State Capitol!

END

Mount Kineo House and Annex on Moosehead Lake, Kineo, Maine, operated by the Ricker Hotel Company, could accommodate 600 guests with "private baths, steam heat and electric lights" as well as tennis, golf, swimming, boating and riding. The hotel opened July 1 for the summer.

GREAT OLD SUMMER HOTELS

Towels with Tassels and Oh, That View

by Edith Mason

In almost every New England town there is someone, usually elderly, who has collected and protected a number of photographs of the community as it was in years gone by. Surprisingly often, when poring through such a collection, one will find oneself lingering over an old, faded photograph of a gigantic, multi-storied structure obviously containing literally hundreds of rooms and adorned with piazzas, balconies, dormers, towers and cupolas.

"That's the old Elmwood Hotel. Burned to the ground two years after that photo was taken," will be the comment—or the name could be Rockmere, Crawford, Leffingwell, New Ocean, Griswold, Mount Pleasant, Clarendon, Chequesset, Hamilton, Nanepashement, Kineo, Passaconaway, Knickerbocker, Prospect, Adams, Ocean View, Lancaster, Waumbek, Fabyan and so many others.

All but forgotten now, these fabulous resorts were where people from all over the country spent their Augusts before the automobile so radically changed America's vacation habits. Families usually went to one particular place year after year, and through decades the new generations came too.

"My grandfather and family went there in

A summer evening on the piazza —
"The orchestra is playing 'Il Trovatore'..."

1875 until 1902," one woman recently wrote us in response to our query about Maine's famous Poland Spring House. "My father and my mother met there," she went on, "and I began going there when I was three months old and for the next 16 years."

There was something for everyone. Father had his golf or tennis, fishing, and skeet shooting; Mother her tea parties, concerts, blueberry picking, and steamer or carriage rides; the children their special game rooms, movies, swimming, camping, horseback riding, or boat excursions.

And as for the young ladies, says one old-time brochure, "romantic nooks abound where a favorite novel and a box of bonbons are cheerful companions, reinforced by ready allies of the masculine persuasion."

In those less hectic times, people also spent many vacation hours doing comparatively nothing. "All afternoon, I've been sitting on the broad verandah that completely encompasses three sides of the hotel and a large part of the fourth," a New York man wrote on the back of a Kineo Hotel postcard. "The orchestra is playing 'Il Trovatore' . . ."

Another postcard talks about the evenings. "The walks in the twilight upon the piazzas, the groups of friends clustered here and there, the admitted privilege of anybody speaking to anybody if he chooses to, the peals of laughter from adjoining rooms . . ."

Mrs. Barbara Bentley, in recalling the old Willoughby Lake House in West Burke, Vermont, says, "The evening gatherings were friendly; card games played by the light of ornately decorated kerosene lamps, and conversation among like-minded students of the arts, sciences or literature, or enjoying peering through the stereoscope at pictures of scenic views of the Vermont countryside."

Still others reminisce about impromptu concerts by talented guests, dancing, and an occasional romantic canoe ride in the moonlight.

"Old men find that they can be young again and young men have the spice and fun of recreation without dissipation," reported the editor

Top: *Gentlemen of the Orchestra off duty pose for their portrait at the Maplewood Hotel in Bethlehem, New Hampshire.* **Bottom:** *Golf in the '90s somewhere in the White Mountains — possibly at the old Mount Pleasant.*

Top: *A lawn tennis party at the Crawford House (N.H.) about 1900.* **Bottom:** *Evening social on the veranda of the Tip-Top House atop Mount Uncanoonuc near Manchester, New Hampshire. Guests ascended to the hotel by cable car.*

Above: The Poland Spring House, billed as "The Leading Resort in New England — Known the World Over," and famous for the purity of its bottled water as well as the scope of its activities, was built by the Ricker family on the old homestead estate of Wentworth Ricker in South Poland, Maine. Homesteader Wentworth opened the first Ricker hotel on the site in 1791 — one of the first to offer "entertainment for man and beast" on the post highway from Portland to Montreal. A 1917 brochure for the Poland Spring explains that "Nearly 120 years of hotel-keeping have evolved the Mansion House, the Poland Spring House, and the Riccar Inn and developed the Estate" (from 300 to 5,000 acres). Families would return year after year to spend the entire month of July or August at this great resort complex, many bringing their own maids, valets and chauffeurs (sometimes their own horses and grooms as well!). The servants were housed at the Riccar Inn.

Right: The Poland Spring House menu for Sunday, August 14th, 1892. You could choose from two kinds of soup; salmon or bluefish for

the fish course; boiled fowl in celery sauce, spring lamb, native duck or sirloin of beef for meats, boiled or roasted; then go on to an entree — potted Philadelphia pigeon, chicken cutlets, Italian fritters or spaghetti in cream — plough through a cold course, salads or boned capon in aspic, nine sorts of vegetables, twelve desserts, three different cheeses, and finish up the meal with tea or coffee.

...the height of solid comfort — and with real cream!

of *New England Magazine* after what surely was an enjoyable visit to the Passaconaway Inn at York Cliffs, Maine, about the turn of the century.

Accommodations were sometimes luxurious —including those with "a long distance telephone in every room" as well as "towels with tassels on them"—but always the height of solid comfort. And of course no one cared about diets.

"The cream, which was served at the table, was skimmed off the top of the pans of milk set in the big pantries after each milking, so that the heavy cream could rise to the top," said Mrs. Bentley.

For all this, you paid anything from $6-7 a week or the same per day—depending upon the place and the year. The Prospect House (once described by Jenny Lind as "The Paradise of America") atop Mount Holyoke advertised

Here's the Jefferson Hill House in Jefferson, New Hampshire, in the days when guests arrived with a month's supply of clothes stuffed in trunks piled atop a stage.

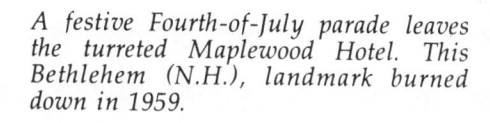

A festive Fourth-of-July parade leaves the turreted Maplewood Hotel. This Bethlehem (N.H.), landmark burned down in 1959.

a night's lodging and breakfast for 38¢. And that included free use of the telescope!

There always seemed to be a view—a fabulous view. Some, like the Prospect House and the Uncanoonuc Inn, were built atop mountains. Guests were taken up to the hotels via specially built cable railroads. Clifton Johnson's Mt. Holyoke Handbook says that everybody who rode the tramway to the Prospect House "considered it a very serious matter and the outcome extremely doubtful. But for a person with steady nerves, the experience was a delightful one." Once at the top, the view was described as "the grandest cultivated view in the world."

A well known writer said of the view at Poland Spring House: "The terraced foothills, the fertile farms that incline along their slope, the little villages tucked away here and there in the distance, the chain of lakes gleaming through the trees, and the shimmering peaks of the New Hampshire mountains known as the Presidential Range, help to make up the picture . . . supremely beautiful at dawn or sunset."

69

...the view is all that's left of most of these grand old places.

The Mount Kineo House (on Moosehead Lake, Kineo, Maine) characterized its own view as "the beauty of one hundred and twenty square miles of sparkling water surrendered to the majesty of the boundless wilds." That the Bunker Hill Monument could be seen from its piazza on a clear day was the proud boast of the Uncanoonuc House of Manchester, New Hampshire.

Today, the view is all that's left of most of these grand old places. Many of them burned down, some were torn down, a few have been converted to other uses. The 1938 Hurricane carried away 60 rooms of the Prospect House, and one or two others have deliberately reduced their size to continue operating.

The SamOset By the Sea, built in 1898 by the Ricker family as a near copy of their Poland Spring House, burned to the ground in 1972 after withstanding years of desolation, and just after it was purchased by a development association for some $875,000 for remodeling into a condominium complex.

The fate of the Poland Spring House was ironically similar. For years the hotel stood empty like a mammoth stage set behind the more modest (only 100 rooms!) modern building called The Inn at Poland Spring, but plans were afoot to reopen the Poland Spring House, together with its adjunct, the Mansion House, by 1980 or before, in a less lavish, more informal style than the Rickers had favored in its heyday. Alas, this was not to be. Like the SamOSet, the Poland Spring House, too, was to go down in flames. The conflagration of July 1975 left nothing but ashes of the grand old hotel.

Nevertheless, a few of New England's huge resort hotels are still (1975) in operation and—with currently increasing demand—offering the elysian amenities of the past. New Hampshire has a number: the Mount Washington Hotel in Bretton Woods; the Mountain View House, Whitefield; The Balsams of Dixville Notch; and Wentworth-by-the-Sea in Portsmouth, whose facilities even include a luxury yacht!

END

1972 — the last days of the once fabulous SamOset By the Sea, built by the Ricker family at Rockland Breakwater, Maine, as a near copy of Poland Spring. The SamOset closed down in 1969.

The Ocean View Hotel on Block Island (R.I.), demolished by flames in 1967.

Emmett Meara photo

L.F. Willard photo

71

Above: *The huge Profile House at Franconia Notch in New Hampshire's White Mountains at the height of its prosperity.* **Below:** *The SamOset By the Sea (see p. 70) ablaze Friday, October 13, 1972. The hotel had been purchased at a price of $875,000 for remodeling into condominiums. Destruction was complete.* **Opposite:** *The Profile House reduced to a single chimney in 1922. This photo was snapped the morning after the fire, when the ruins were still smouldering. Note the smoke rising just behind the chimney.*

Courtesy *The Courier-Gazette* — Raymond E. Gross photo

Courtesy Frank Hussey

END

Covered Wagons in the Yard
by Margo Holden

The wagons would erupt with kids scattering in all directions — to the barn, the henhouse, the garden, the orchard...

As I recall, 1919 saw the last of the gypsy caravans. They would pass through Jackman, Maine, making the trek from points north down through the New England states to warmer climates for the winter, swing west and then north, entering Canada somewhere around Lake Erie, and thence come round round again. That would take two or three years.

They were a colorful lot, these caravans. They usually traveled in groups of three wagons—covered wagons, that is. Each wagon contained from seven to eleven gypsies of all ages. The wagons were drawn by two horses each, and the horses were the best-looking part of their outfit. Evidently, the gypsies took great pride in them. They seemed always to be black horses, brushed, sleek, and well fed. Their harnesses were oiled, tended, and bejeweled, the brow bands carrying rosettes of bright colored wool.

Some summers we would have only one visit from them, but usually there were two or three caravans in the course of a summer. They lived off the land along the way and were real professional pilferers, scavengers, and beggars. Cleanliness was not one of their faults.

Perhaps if I could have eavesdropped on some of their campfires of an evening and listened to their fabled guitars and accordions or heard their voices singing the strange wild songs attributed to them or watched their dancing, I might have retained a more romantic memory of these gypsies. Or could I have lived with them I might give a more lenient report. Surely other than their unorthodox method of procuring a livelihood and their roaming way of living, they probably were a decent lot.

What became of the gypsies, anyway? People have conjectured that the younger generation preferred to be like other young folk in normal communities, while the older generation probably got jobs with the circus. Unless they traveled as a tight social family group, they could not make that way of life pay off. No one welcomed them. They were run off a place or out of town as soon as the surprised "host" could manage it.

This surprise element was one of their tactics. Our family on a farm in Dennistown, north of Jackman, would be still grumbling weeks after a visit from the last gypsy caravan when we would hear the dogs barking. It would be such a sudden uproar and sound like the hounds of Baskerville pitched against the wolves of Siberia. Rushing outdoors, we would see two or three covered wagons pulled up in the yard. The wagons would fairly erupt with kids scattering in all directions: some to the barn to snitch all the eggs and as many hens as they could catch; some to the orchard; some to the garden. The adults would disembark and disperse about as rapidly and as cleverly. One would go to the wagon shed, a couple to the garden, and about three to the house. One would run around to the back door where the woodshed was; two would come in the front door.

I remember once there was this old crone who buckled on to my grandfather who was coming in to dinner and insisted on telling his fortune, all the time trying to get at his wallet which he kept in his shirt pocket, fastened by a large safety pin. My grandmother, who was in the kitchen, was hard put to fence off the two who were in there. She was turning sausage in the skillet, using a large butcher knife which she brandished at a hag who was trying to beg the sausage from her. My grandmother could hear the fellow in the shed rummaging around. She

GYPSIES

Gypsy caravans usually traveled in groups of three wagons. Many a New Englander remembers well the hectic occasions of their visits — once every two or three years.

could see the other one who had come in the front door now in the cupboard under the stairs where food was kept, secreting jars of jam in her pockets. The fortune teller was holding my grandfather by the suspenders with one hand, her face about two inches from his, telling him what a nice man he was, and with the other hand she had the safety pin unfastened. That was when my grandmother saw what was going on through the open door. She let out a whoop that would do credit to a mother bear.

"You take your hands off him," she cried, "I'm going to get the gun and shoot every last one of you!"

In the confusion that followed, the old hag got the sausage, pan and all. When my grandmother returned from getting the gun, the gypsies were all piling into the wagons. In fact the lead wagon had already started down the hill.

The whole shebang lasted only about ten minutes. But what an uproarious hullabaloo! Everybody shouting orders to everybody else in a tongue we didn't understand. Their dogs and our dogs fighting it out, barking and snarling in seven different languages, it seemed. Even the horses neighed and stamped with the excitement. Hens ran around squawking and trying to keep from being caught by the kids pursuing them, who were in turn screaming at the top of their lungs. Oh, it was a glorious fracas! And then they would leave as quickly as they had come. The funny part was we would never hear them arriving.

Back in those days on the farm, we had few visitors come by and the advent of any visitor would give us something to talk about for days. But a visit from a bunch of gypsies was memorable. Looking back, I think I rather relished all the excitement. The gypsies would nearly clean us out though. I remember all we had for dinner once after they had left were the biscuits which they didn't know were in the oven. END

A Rigorous and Gentle Art

by John Chase

"Stowing" hay into the far corners of the hayloft way up
in top of the barn on a hot July day is no picnic!

HAYING

Vermont, around the turn of the century.

There is no doubt that from one locality in New England to another, or even from one farm to another, there would be differences in the methods of haying during the early 20th century. Basically, however, these processes would apply to the typical, one-horse farm. This refers to the time when machinery was first making its appearance, and the pieces mentioned could be found on almost any farmstead.

We all know that the first step is to cut the growing grass. This was done in the open fields with the horse-drawn machine. Width of the cut was 3½ feet: 42 inches if you were able to guide the apparatus at 100 percent efficiency. But bear in mind that the machine was drawn by a horse who might weave from side to side a foot or so if you did not pay close attention. Also keep in mind that the machine was made of cast iron and therefore was very brittle. Once broken, you were completely and irrevocably out of business; you could not just call the shop and have them send over a welder. So, you kept a wide berth around any obstacles such as trees and stone walls. Anything that you did not cut with the machine had to be mowed with a hand scythe.

The horse could only stand this sort of work for three or, at the most, four hours. Then, while he was having a deserved rest and a long lunch hour, the human part of the team could

About six acres of field needed to be cut per cow.

Before the advent of horse-drawn machinery, mowing, raking, turning and bunching were all done by hand.

sharpen the mower knives. This job, alone, with a foot-pedaled grindstone was something to try the patience of almost anyone. If a wife, neighbor or some unsuspecting child could be conned into turning the stone it made the job very much easier. A little company was nice too. With help, you might even get the hand scythe ground at the same time. This sharpening would be a daily chore until the last of the hay was cut.

All "spare" time was devoted to hand mowing with the scythe, much of the work being done in the early morning while the grass was still wet and the horse was eating his breakfast.

Hand mowing ("trimming") was important for at least two reasons: one, most of the hay was "old field" and only from 12 to 16 inches in height, but every spear and blade of it was needed; and two, if the edges of the fields were not kept trimmed constantly each year, nature would soon reclaim her own—first with bushes, then with trees. It is unlikely there would be more than one-half ton of hay on an acre. The rough estimate in my boyhood neighborhood was three tons to feed a cow through the winter. So, about six acres of field needed to be cut per cow. For a horse, it depended somewhat on his size and how hard he would be worked through the winter, but generally, about the same figure could be used as a fair average.

Lunch over, and back to the hay field. With the horse now harnessed to the next piece of mechanical equipment, a "horse rake," the hay cut in the morning was raked into "winrows." (The dictionary spells it "windrows.") This

Above: *Hay being pitched and treaded down to "build" a load.* **Below:** *Scythes had to be sharpened regularly during haying time — several times a day, the number of times depended on the type of grass being cut.*

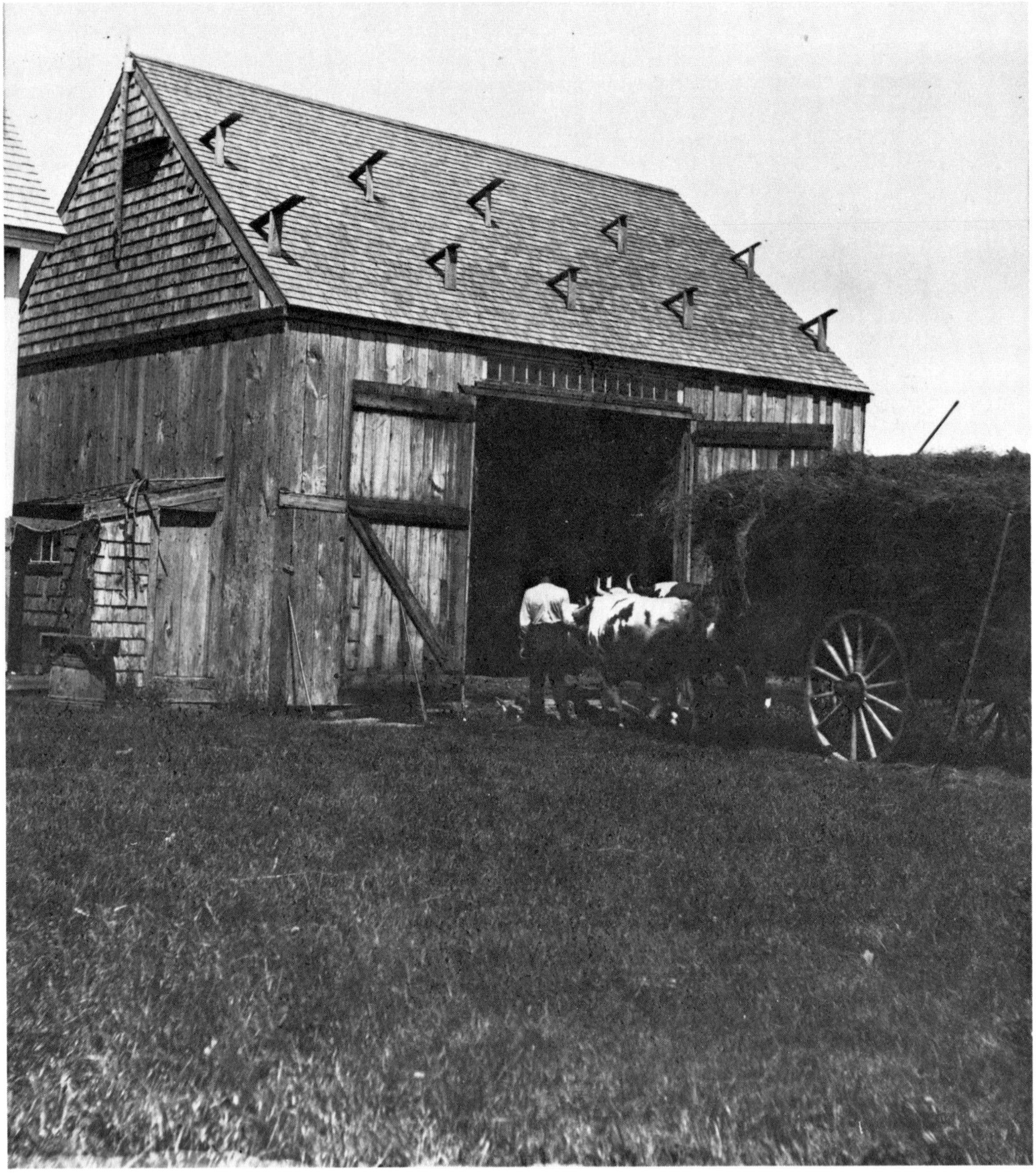

Bunching hay so that very little rain could penetrate it was an art in itself.

went much faster than the mowing as the rake would be about eight feet in width. With the raking done for the day, the horse could, at least on the first day, rest until the following morning. For the farmer, it was next necessary to "bunch" the hay. This meant piling it up in bunches or, as called by city folks, "hay cocks." Bunching hay was an art in itself. A good man could bunch so that even on a rainy day very little water would penetrate the pile. It also made the next day's operations easier.

The following day, more mowing in the morning until all the dew had dried on the ground. When the ground was dry, the bunches had to be "shook out." This meant spreading the hay around on the ground so that it could dry. After two hours or so, depending on the type of day and the heat of the sun, the hay had to be "turned." This meant getting what was on the ground up to the air and on a different spot on the field. Moisture will gather under a pile of hay even on the fairest day. "Opening" the bunches was a lot easier when it had been properly bunched the day before. Later in the day, if not sufficiently well dried and suitable to be "put in" the barn, it would be bunched up again for the night.

Almost no one put hay in a barn the same day it was cut. The danger of fire from spontaneous combustion sometime later was just too great to risk. If there is any moisture in hay, it will generate a tremendous amount of heat. If it does not create an open fire and burn the barn, it will most assuredly spoil the hay. Many farmers used to add salt to the hay in the mow to reduce the danger of fire. Whether it worked or not is not for me to judge.

The morning's mowing had to be raked and bunched. This continued every day until the mowing was complete. Each day there was more to bunch, shake out and turn until some of it was ready for the barn. All this turning, tossing and shaking was so the hay would "make." When ready for storage in the barn, it was "made."

After about the third day, the first of the cutting was ready to be "put in." The horse was "hooked" to the "hayrack." Here, one person was a pretty poor crew. As the hay was quite loose and fluffy, it did not take very much to fill the rack. With a second person in the rack to "tread" and "build" the load, four or five times as much could be taken at one trip. This hauling in was not nearly so hard on the horse as mowing or raking, as it only had to go from one bunch to another, then rest while the hay was pitched on the rack. For the few minutes it took to go from the field to the barn, the human element could ride and rest.

A word or two about the rack is in order. This was a container, for want of a better word, from 16 to 20 feet in length, depending upon the builder's enthusiasm and the materials available. The bottom would be more or less a standard three feet wide as it did have to fit between the wheels. Near the front there were V-shaped gashes cut in the floor to make a place for the wheels when the rack made a turn. The front axle, being rigid, caused one wheel to go forward when turning and the other to go to the rear and toward the center of whatever was following. The sides sloped outward to make a width at the top of five or six feet. The rail at the top was held up by stakes or peeled poles approximately one inch in diameter and spaced about one foot apart. Sides would vary in height, but four feet would be an average—the whole making a light but strong device.

Most every farm had a cart of some sort. These would consist of a pair of front wheels and a pair of rear wheels connected by a "reach." To use the hay rack, the reach was extended to whatever length best fit the rack. If the reach would not naturally adjust to the length needed, a pole, plank or something could be lashed in to hold the axles apart and a chain put from front to back so that the front would haul the rear. This was in turn hauled by the horse, not, as some may say, "by the shafts." The shafts did not haul anything. The primary purpose of the shafts was to give leverage for turning and for holding back or backing up. Pulling was from the horse by way of "tugs" which were hooked to a "whiffletree" which in turn was bolted, chained or otherwise securely fastened to the front axle.

"Pitching it off" meant taking the hay from the rack and putting it on the "mow," which in most barns meant from two to six feet above your head. Here again a great deal of time-consuming labor was saved if there was another person to "take away" and "stow." "Stowing" was getting the hay back in the far corners of the barn and piling it so that there would be a place to unload the next rackful. Up in the top of a barn on a hot July day, stowing hay, believe me, is no picnic.

One other little chore was raking "scatterings." When the hay was picked up in the fields and loaded on the rack, some was bound to be left that the pitchfork would not pick up. This had to be raked by hand. Some farmers used a small wooden hand rake while others had a loafer rake. The loafer was a larger, also wooden, rake about four feet in width. A good industrious "loafer," if he kept nearly on the run, could hold his own with whoever was loading and leave the field clean behind them.

Finally the last load would be in. The mower would be stored away somewhere in a building. These must have been either very expensive or otherwise very hard to come by. Rarely do I know of one being left outside through the winter. True, they did not take up anywhere near as much room as a rake. They were one of the few specialized pieces of equipment anywhere on the farm. After mowing there was no other use for them all the rest of the year.

The rake, on the other hand, especially the later models which were all metal, were many times left right where they were last unhooked. The rack body, finally emptied of its last load, would be taken from the wheels and hoisted to the top of the barn, there to be used as a storage place for beans when their turn came for harvesting. The wheels would go back in service again for the various other farm duties. The haying was done, and the farmer could stop for a few brief moments to gaze with satisfaction on a full storehouse of winter food for his animals.

END

by Ned Brown and Frank W. Lovering

Time was in coastal New England when farmers whose land ran to tidewater went out on the marsh each fall with a yellow-backed *Old Farmer's Almanac(k)* in one hand, scythe snath cradled under armpit or over sturdy shoulder, and whetstone in overalls pocket.

Their going was no gamble. The marsh must be hayed then in a mass movement, or never that year. The wild salt grass could only be worked on neap tide, lowest in the lunar month, and the *Almanac(k)* gave the signal for the onslaught in its fine-type table of the tides.

Each patch of salt meadow was reached by an ancient right of way. The best of the crop, if carefully harvested at the proper season, made a valuable fodder for cattle. The "proper season" was when the moon was in its first or third quarter. Thus the unusually low tide favored the work.

Shore farmers ordinarily sold their salt hay for fodder and used the regular "English" hay for their own stock. Hay and grain dealers seldom handle salt hay for fodder now, but nevertheless cattle often are to be seen grazing knee-high in tidewater grass. The animals love it, although today scientists say it is an inferior roughage with nutrient value not over half as much per ton as upland hay. Frequently the two were mixed for stock feed.

Salt hay is softer and finer than ordinary sweet hay. The choicest variety, called "black grass," is dark brown in hue, and especially desired as bedding, winter feed for cattle, and for mulching because it does not leave a deposit of grass seed in gardens. It is used particularly to cover strawberry and parsnip beds. Roadbuilders like it, too, for use on roadsides to prevent erosion. It was grown, cut, and stored in stacks on the tidewater marshes which stretch from the mouth of Newbury's Parker River to the Merrimac River, and east, from Plum Island River to the mainland of Rowley, and to Newburyport on the west. The land is low and flat and, on a high run of tide, completely covered with salt water. Thus, the trend of the tide was important to the salt hay farmer.

Salt hay on a staddle, Plum Island, Mass.

Many years ago, drainage ditches were dug to help the natural run-off of water. In late August or September, the farmer would hitch up his horses, pile the hay wagons with his hired men, and head for the marshes. In order that the horses might not sink into the ooze of the marshes, they were fitted with bog (or clog) shoes—platforms about a foot square. (Even with this protection, a horse might get caught in an extremely soft spot.) The shoes were commonly made in farm shops during the winter. Sections of plank were fitted with blocks and straps, or with wires attached to leather bands which were buckled fast near the fetlock of each leg of the animal. The toe of the horseshoe was adapted to the shape of the hoof.

Plank marsh shoes were clumsy, and inventors soon designed several types from iron which found wide sale. These were latticed in one pattern or another to prevent the horse's feet from sinking into the soft ground. Methods of affixing the shoe were ingenious. They ranged from a clamp against the rear calks which, when set up with a wrench forced the toe into the arch fashioned for the hoof, to a shoe with slots in two lateral arms. When the bolts on the latter were tightened they held the toe firmly in a band that received the front calk.

The hazard to horses here described was not the only one experienced on a trip into the marshes. They had to be fitted with straw hats and net hangings, to "keep the greenhead flies from pestering them to death," as one farmer described it.

The haymakers wore wide-brimmed hats and, along with their lunch, carried jugs of liquid refreshment to allay the tedium and rigors of their task.

Salt hay was cut, raked, and stored on stilts, or staddles, to protect it from future high tides until such time in the winter as the marshes are frozen over. Then the farmers went into action again. In the days before mechanical equipment, they depended upon heavy hay pungs. The flat, hefty sleds were fitted with side slats for holding the hay load. Pungs would usually make the trip in groups, for everyone's safety and in order that the task might not be lonely. Each pung had an enclosed vestibule that protected the driver on the long, cold ride.

Sometimes the hay was loaded right onto gundalows or barges and towed away by sea, if the meadow permitted easy access from the water.

Though salt haying has not existed as a large-scale industry since the turn of the century, memorials to it remain. The marshes of New England's five coastal states, and of New York and New Jersey, are studded with staddles, the curious but serviceable support for the salt hay stacks, which held the mounded and curing hay above the highest normal tides. In spring, the circles of red cedar sticks stand gaunt above the new marsh grass, a puzzle to passing travelers, but as the grass grows tall in high summer, rippling in the vagrant breeze, the staddles sink out of sight to be forgotten once again.   END

Beacon Hill garden, fall, 1927.

BEACON HILL

The Hub of the Universe

by Frances Minturn Howard

Where eccentricities are merely "habits," "lavish" is a dirty word, and houses are never overheated...

When I first came to Boston I was dogged by a series of haunting sayings—tag ends of sentences which lodged disturbingly in my mind. The remark of our hostess's husband, for example, who politely saw us out one day after tea. As we said goodbye, I happened to comment on an interesting old painting—a Primitive, really—I had seen upstairs.

"My wife's mother was a Primitive," our host observed, meditatively.

And out we floated into the dark.

Another provocative comment came from an elderly neighbor, describing the husband of a friend. "*Was* he eccentric? He had toes sewed in his socks."

Eccentricities are usually, however, not called so in Boston; they are merely habits, stoutly defended.

"But why *shouldn't* she have herself listed in the telephone book in the name of a tree? All her *friends* know what tree to call."

There were other phrases like, "She lives on the Wrong Side of the Hill."

The Wrong Side—obviously not the place to be, but what penalties were attached? Where was the dividing line drawn?

There was, one day, a great display of shiny, red fire engines in front of a certain house on Chestnut Street. "Oh," said a friend I was walking with, without any special interest, "I imagine it's just Letitia Allen's Annual Fire."

"Does she have a fire every year?"

"*Practically* every year. She missed last."

Buying an old house on Beacon Hill is equivalent, immediately, to a new education. You learn things from your neighbors, your in-laws, the policemen, the fire department—practically everyone is willing to instruct you. The janitors on Beacon Hill who come to take out your ash barrels biweekly and polish your

A bathtub on the sidewalk at seven in the morning is not an uncommon sight.

brass doorknobs are reticent, courteous men who will not force their information on you, but they have it. Our first was a light-colored, cheerful fellow who wore a black beret dashingly on one side of his head; it took me some time to discover that he also spoke fluent Greek.

Mr. O'Malley, our first Hill policeman, was a liberal source of information in himself. If you met him walking up The Hill in the morning, you could kiss goodbye to at least a half hour of your day. But it was worth it. Mr. O'Malley was a living encyclopedia; he was familiar with every family on Beacon Hill—where they lived and what their reputation was. He was courteous with strangers, but I think he bristled a little, like a faithful dog, at the sight of one.

Mr. O'Malley had his own way of checking up on things. He did not barge in; he infiltrated. I was lying out in a long chair in our little back garden one fine spring day, reading, when finding myself suddenly in the shade, I looked up to see the not-inconsiderable bulk of Mr. O'Malley outlined against the sun. The passageway door to the street had been left open, and Mr. O'Malley had come in by it. He was, he explained (for Mr. O'Malley never did anything out of vulgar curiosity; he always had a reason), "taking a look around for some police horses."

"Horses?" I said vaguely. "Oh, I don't think we could get any in here; the passageway is too narrow."

I thus revealed my ignorance. Mr. O'Malley meant, he explained, those wooden sawhorses placed in front of houses to reserve space for some emergency.

Our neighbors, an attractive young couple who had turned to and painted the front hall of their house a pale apple-green, were even more startled when Mr. O'Malley suddenly popped up beside them in their walnut-

Lamplighter at work on the Hill, late 1920s.

...hot chocolate in a great china pot with whipped cream; tea and coffee; paper-thin asparagus sandwiches, cookies, cakes, and plates of vanilla ice cream with huge ripe strawberries...

panelled library. They had been lounging there, exhausted, over a revivifying can of beer. (Again, the front door had been left open, to air out the smell of paint.)

"Well," said Mr. O'Malley, looking around at the walnut panelling of the library, "thank God you didn't paint *this* anyway."

I made a most unfortunate social error early in my acquaintance with Mr. O'Malley; I gave a largish party and didn't invite him. But Mr. O'Malley was a big man, and he forgave me. He knew it was not ill will on my part, but simply ignorance. He came anyway.

His excuse for appearing was a large City Directory which he had promised one of the guests, the literary editor of a book review section of the newspaper; naturally, it had to be delivered there and then. Mr. O'Malley was introduced to the guest of honor, an author in whose works, it seemed, he took an interest; he then departed. I was not so inept again.

One of the first things that strikes a stranger in Boston about Beacon Hill is the odd times plumbing is done. To see a bathtub sitting out in the street at seven in the morning is a not uncommon sight. The fact is, all the old houses on Beacon Hill are so full of Violations that it is merely a question of whether an inspector wishes to clap one on or not. Fire escapes wander crazily from one house to another. Retaining walls, common to two contiguous houses but the sole property of neither, are a fruitful source of guerrilla combat. It is common knowledge that all improvements are noted with a jealous eye by Big Brother, the Tax Collector, and this is why you will see new bathtubs sitting outside on the curb before breakfast, to be rushed inside and installed before any inspectors are stirring.

I spent my first two years in Boston freezing to death. New York is a steam-heated place; Boston is not. I used to sit, on those rare occasions when we were invited out to dinner, trying not to hug my bare shoulders and speculating wildly on what kind of undergarments the other guests could be wearing that enabled them to sit, apparently, in comfort.

Certain people, I felt, carried this to extremes. At one of my first Reading Club afternoons I was astonished to see everybody, the moment we were let in the door by the uniformed maid, rush to a large pile of old sweaters, coats, and army blankets laid out helter-skelter on a handsome carved chair in the hall, and hastily climb into them. While I was still wondering at this, I began to shiver uncontrollably. The great, superbly furnished house, floor-to-ceiling tapestried and riddled with imposing marble statuary, was as unheated as a storage vault.

We sat on the second floor huddled as near as possible to a small fire, our borrowed sweaters swathing our goose-pimpled shoulders, while we listened for an hour and a half to the reading of the day's book. My teeth were chattering like castanets; I feared they could be heard above the reading.

Our hostess said to me, kindly, that she hoped I wouldn't be chilly; she did not care for overheated houses. She did not care for taxis either, I heard later. When she and her very distinguished brother were invited out to dinner, *he* went by taxi while *she* went by streetcar. Yet she gave vast sums to her favorite charities.

This combination of extreme personal thrift and public benevolence is a not uncommon Boston trait. A strong Puritan heritage may account for it. It isn't that Bostonians don't enjoy a good tuck-in as well as the next one. Nobody can lay in food and drink with more relish than your good Bostonian, if somebody else is paying for it. But don't expect either gratitude or appreciation from the recipients. They reserve the right, while lapping up food and drink with the gusto of a professional pie-eater, to look down their noses at the host setting out such a spread.

"Lavish" is a dirty word in Boston.

Not long after my arrival I became entangled in a series of Sunday Afternoon Teas given by an elderly neighbor. I was never really sure why she asked me; we disagreed on every conceivable subject. But indulging her own perversities had become her great amusement. She enjoyed an argument. She would seat perhaps a dozen suitably conservative people around her large tea table and then throw out some remark like, "I feel we have been being *unreasonably rude* to the poor dear Russians." She would then sit back and bask in the fireworks.

To be asked to serve tea was a dubious honor; you starved. The antique silver teapot was a beautiful little piece, holding perhaps a pint of hot liquid at one time. You served three or four people, and then the maid, almost as antique as the pot, limped slowly downstairs to some subterranean hideout to fetch more. By the time she got back, the first-served had drunk their tea and were impatiently in line with the ones who hadn't had any yet. You never got any refreshment yourself, and went home parched.

Our hostess never noticed; she was supremely indifferent to any material comfort. Yet everything in the house was unique of its kind, like the exquisite little mahogany chairs people dragged up to the tea table.

I was unfortunately not present on the day a large and dignified lady sat down on one and went through to the floor, but the scene was graphically described to me. The lady was hauled up by two gallant gentlemen who had difficulty extricating her, since her far-from-scanty nether portions had become firmly embedded in the seat of her splintered chair.

These teas paled beside the first Literary one I attended on Beacon Hill. In every literary gathering I had up to now attended, literature came first, tea later; it being a well understood, if seldom mentioned, fact that food and drink are always dispensed as a sort of reward for those who have stuck bravely by through the intellectual part of the afternoon.

Not here. Here, the order was courageously reversed. We were taken down one flight to a basement dining room where a stupendous High Tea had been set out. There was hot chocolate in a great, wonderful, china pot, with whipped cream; tea and coffee; paper-thin asparagus sandwiches, cookies, cakes, and plates of vanilla ice cream with huge ripe strawberries to be consumed as a sort of Crowning Touch to this magnificent supper—for supper it really was. This was such fare as poets seldom enjoy.

Skinny, ancient maids in immaculate uniforms darted about the room bearing trays of sandwiches and ice cream, urging more food on the not reluctant guests. I remember vividly one especially Mary Petty maid, her starched apron strings flying, scooching down with a plate of strawberries and ice cream under the hand of two gesticulating people and emerging triumphantly on the other side, her burden intact.

Fed, replete, and bursting at the seams with goodies, the entire party then ascended to the main floor. The inside wooden shutters, painted a dark gold, had been closed, leaving the old-fashioned double parlors in poetic cathedral gloom. Sitting about carelessly on lacquer tables were large hunks of raw amethyst, figurines, superb little mother-of-pearl bibelots. From one wall protruded the head and neck of a large antique swan, possibly Florentine, of finely carved and painted white wood. On another hung a full-length Sargent portrait of our hostess.

It was she who opened the proceedings. In her eighties, still beautiful, standing before us she read, without the aid of eyeglasses, from some of her favorite ancient philosophers. She could have filled any theater with her exquisitely modulated voice.

After this the poetry reading took place. Came the poetry; large doses of it; and not one person defected! No one took the opportunity to slip out! Truly, I began to see that Bostonians are cut from different stuff.

Once a year the little backyard gardens on Beacon Hill are opened, at a small price, for a Garden Tour which the public may attend. I

...a casual array of her own

was surprised to hear this event spoken of scornfully by the same lady who dispensed with heat in her house.

"Oh, not for me! All this rushing out at the last minute to stick a milk bottle with a daffodil in it in the ground!"

It was hardly a just comment; but there was, I found, a reason for her bitterness towards garden showing. Years before, at a time when things were far more decorous than they are today, she had unwittingly caused a considerable scandal in Garden Club circles. Captivated by the gay informality of the little vine-covered gardens of Italy, she decided to reproduce in her Beacon Hill garden some of this wayward European charm. She therefore caused long clotheslines to be strung out over her garden and, just before the Annual Tour of garden-lovers arrived, she ordered hung up on the lines a casual array of her own immaculately laundered undergarments.

It was meant to be a reproduction of a gay, informal Neapolitan scene; but somehow, in Boston, the effect was not quite the same. Moving about under a flapping cloud of Mrs. C.'s skivvies, Beacon Hill visitors felt distinctly ill at ease. Were you supposed to look? How could you *not* look?

It made history.

The Waltz Evenings are a great Boston Institution, open to those socially eligible and terpsichorially fit. We had the honor, shortly after our arrival in Boston, to be invited to one. Our host, a charming fellow in his early eighties (many of Boston's most delightful hosts are in their early eighties), was a skilled and inveterate waltzer. If my remembrance of the evening is not quite the glowing one I had anticipated, it is perhaps because of the very proficiency of our host.

His method of dancing was to pick out a small, not-too-frequented spot on the floor with the care of a male Whooping Crane selecting a favorable nesting-site, and then, without ever leaving it, to revolve with increasing rapidity on this spot, like a top shot from a string. As we spun rapidly round and round, I could only try, whirling on my fractured toes, to keep my balance and stay on my feet. I had a terrifying vision of myself crashing to the floor in an unseemly tangle with my elderly cavalier, and I could imagine the uncharitable guesses made in this case by the other dancers on the amount of champagne I had presumably consumed to cause this catastrophe.

It seemed to me that my partner's gyrations, far from running down, increased in velocity as we went along. I felt that to others we must appear as a sort of imposing joint blur, like the blades of an aeroplane propeller. Was

immaculately laundered undergarments.

he carried along by the sheer force of his own momentum? Could he perhaps (the terrifying thought came to me suddenly) *not* stop?

Suddenly it was over. The music mercifully stopped. Perfectly calm, in full possession of his breath, our host said pleasantly, "Ah, there is Mrs. Galway. We must go over and speak to her."

I made my way beside him with a noticeable lurch in my gait. What she thought of me I shall never know; but I have the distinct impression that Mrs. Galway had two heads.

The Boston Symphony is one of the world's finest. But when I first came to Boston I was puzzled by the fact that on certain Fridays two or three people would call up to offer me their Symphony tickets; on other days, not a single one. It must, I thought, be accident; yet it was odd how often it happened.

It took me a little time, and not a few soakings, to discover that Bostonians read the weather reports with the attention with which others peruse astrological charts. On the day when a severe blizzard with four to six inches of heavy snowfall is predicted, a generous rain of symphony tickets may be expected.

On one such afternoon, spent ensconced in somebody else's seat, I found on emerging that a really violent storm was raging; driving snow, howling winds, gusts of gale force. Even the M.T.A. was not running; a line of several hundred waiting people extended all the way out to the street. I wrapped my coat around me, shut my useless umbrella, and set out to walk home.

The stinging snow and hail blinded me, gale-force winds forced me to bend double, my rain hood was precious little protection. Reaching Beacon Hill at last, I struggled up it, proud of my rugged valor. And saw coming towards me an elderly lady in, at least, her late seventies, who lives near me.

"I just walked back from the *symphony!*" I shouted above the roar of the elements.

"Yes, so did I," she said casually. "Bracing, isn't it?"

I crept home, deflated.

One of the favorite indoor sports on Beacon Hill is attending Civic Association meetings to discuss neighborhood matters—a bridge, a turn-around, a new one-way street. These are definitely not to be missed. To see the adjoining citizenry streaking down to the Meeting House for one of these evening affairs, walking single file like Indians on the warpath, brows bent, eyes glittering with purpose, is to realize Trouble is Brewing. The fact is, these neighborhood meetings are the modern equivalent of The Bear Pit. All is likely to go deceptively well

A visit from the nuns and a horse-drawn Victoria in Louisburg Square, probably about 1900.

...a red-faced gentleman, trembling with rage...

A sunny morning on Beacon Hill in the Twenties.

for the Speaker until, lulled into a false sense of security by the truly flattering attention with which his words have been received, he winds up his address and asks if there are any questions.

Are there any questions! Long, long will he rue the day that he asked that one. Aside from an engraving of Custer's Last Stand, there is little to describe the ensuing scene. The inhabitants of Beacon Hill move in for the scalping en masse. Questions are shot at the Speaker from all sections of the floor, some from persons seated, some standing. Agitated hands, clamoring for attention, beat in the air like storm-tossed weather vanes.

The gentleman with the loudest voice usually gets the floor first. He has what is technically a question; but it manages to cast aspersions on the Speaker's integrity, knowledge, education, and intentions.

The fact is, the residents of Beacon Hill, with a cunning born of long years of heckling at Civic Meetings, are experts at asking what purports to be a question while constituting a masterful rebuttal of everything the Speaker has said. Since questions have been invited, there is no way, short of lassoing the questioner and dragging him bodily off the floor, that the Speaker can silence him; and meanwhile the lady on his right is furiously signalling to be heard, and in the back of her a red-faced gentleman is on his feet, trembling with rage, and on the other side of the aisle . . .

Afterwards, while the unfortunate Speaker is still wondering what hit him, refreshments are served in the basement. Virtuously thirsty from the public airing of their own ideas, Beacon Hillers lap up quarts of orange drink and coffee while chewing and spitting out bits of the Speaker. A thoroughly enjoyable time has been had by all, and nobody can wait for the next meeting.

No, Boston is never dull. It is not a place, like New York, where pleasure is a duty; but you would have to go a long way to find people more adept at turning duty into pleasure. END

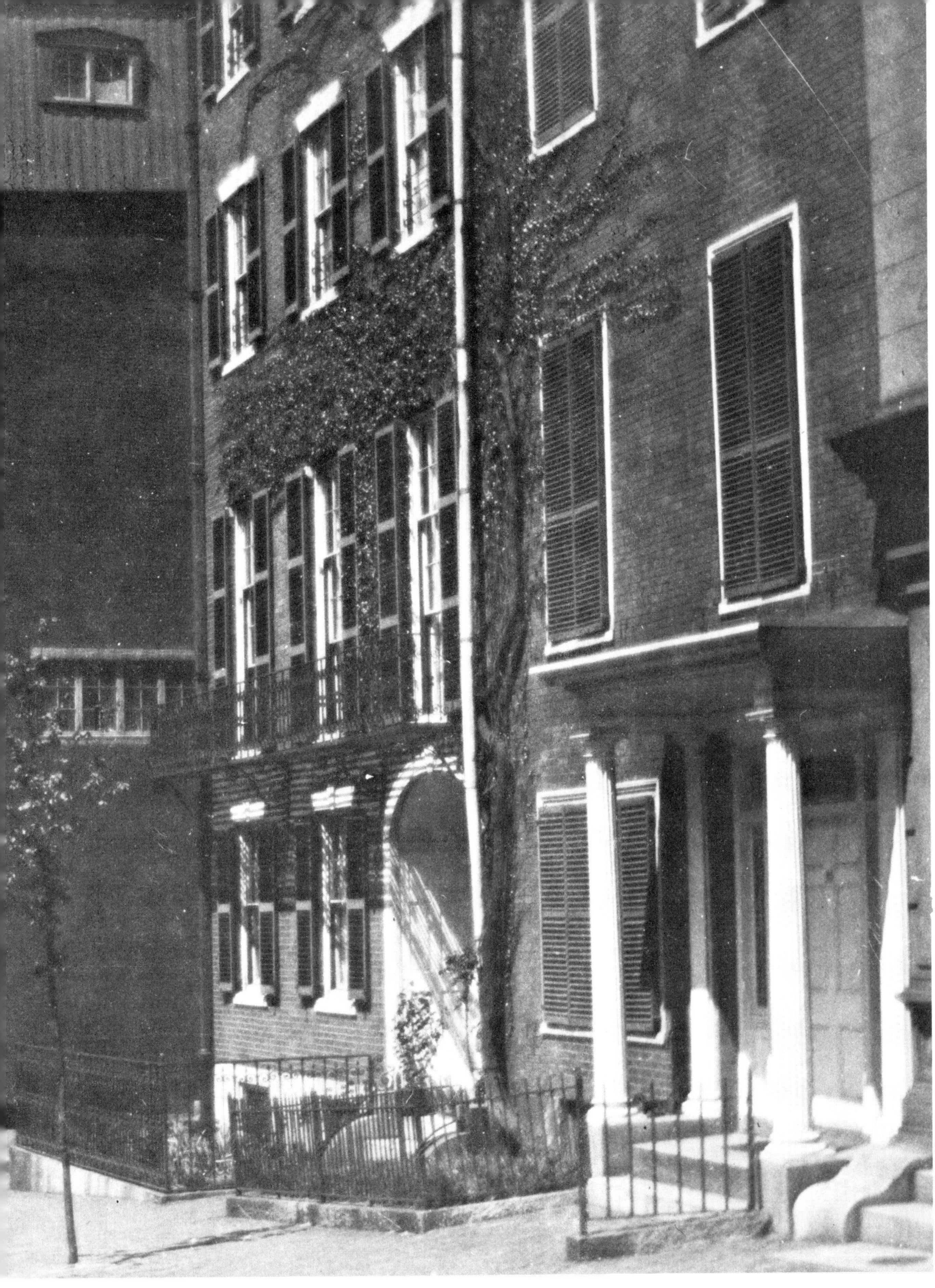

Waste Not, Want Not

by Pauline L. Jensen

Not one iota of God-given manna was wasted — including eggshells and peach peelings.

THRIFT

It was from Aunt Martha that we learned a valuable lesson in thrift. "Waste not, want not," was engraved upon a plaque in her kitchen, and it was also deeply ingrained in her heart.

A product of New England, Aunt Martha lived in an era when the garden vegetables made a one-way trek either to the table or the glass jar. It was her desire that not one iota of God-given manna be wasted. Take potatoes, for instance. When the new potatoes made their appearance, they were scraped, and a peck of potatoes yielded up about two cups of scrapings. These, with the breakfast egg shells, were dried and reduced to particles, and went back to the ground via the earth around the cucumber vines.

In late summer, when the potatoes were too thick-skinned to scrape, they were boiled with the "jackets" on and eaten as was. In winter they were baked, or on occasion, peeled carefully, with the eyes lifted out, not cut. Aunt Martha was a past master at denuding a potato with the resulting waste nil.

Celery leaves, plus the tops of early spring onions, were chopped and dried and placed in a tight container for use in the winter soups. Cucumbers were never peeled, but sliced thin and eaten with relish even by those who were sure they'd end up with Cholera Morbus.

String beans reached the table all of a size, being garnered in their adolescence rather than in childhood. This insured the maximum production from each vine. Beet tops furnished the necessity "greens" and the beets were served buttered, or went to the jars as pickles. The stalks chopped and dried were returned to the ground in the form of nourishment for the late pole beans.

Since it was a time-honored custom to bake apple pies minus the peelings, Aunt Martha tossed the skins into a kettle, boiled them with a little water, strained the resulting juice and put it aside to be used when the raspberry and chokecherry jelly was to be made. This eliminated the cost of store-packaged pectins and, in Aunt Martha's opinion (shared by many), produced a finer jelly than any store pectin. Peach peelings were set aside, and with the peaches too soft to can were cooked, sieved, and made into peach butter that had a flavor never equaled elsewhere.

Peach pits, cherry seeds and apricot stones were set aside to dry, and used in conjunction with the firewood for the winter.

Aunt Martha had a passion for corn, and nary a kernel was disposed of wantonly. Corn left from a meal was cut from the cobs, blanched, and then placed on a clean board, covered with mosquito netting and put to dry in the sun. This brought forth during the winter and cooked with rich milk and butter was indeed a tasty dish. Needless to say, the cobs and husks served their purpose, too, in supplementing the winter fuel.

Soap-making was another of Aunt Martha's accomplishments. She saved every teaspoon of grease, and carefully sieved and set aside wood ashes. Just what purpose these served in relation to each other, plus the lye that was added, was never quite clear,* but ultimately she produced huge bars of soap which, applied to the human body, peeled the skin right down to flesh! It did have its merits, however, for Aunt Martha's wash was the envy of every housewife in town. For guests there were "store-bought" cakes, which, hopefully, would be used in sufficient, but certainly not lavish quantities.

Aunt Martha had a brother, Bill. His wife died, and following the receipt of her insurance, he spent a year in Florida. Ever mindful of his sister, he sent her in good time a bushel each of oranges, grapefruit, and lemons.

The family chuckled, and wondered how she would dispose of the rinds. Cagily, Aunt Martha retained possession of her windfall, and although guests were treated to an occasional orange or a glass of lemonade, no fruit went beyond the confines of her kitchen.

Throughout the year Aunt Martha saved every scrap of ribbon and bits of tissue paper. Those, ironed and freshened, made her Christmas packages stand out. The year of the big windfall from Florida, in each pretty package was a year's supply of marmalade! Aunt Martha had met another challenge and given us a gift of thrift.

END

*Soapmaking is explained in *The Forgotten Arts*, Book One, by Richard M. Bacon, published by Yankee, Inc., 1975 ($2.50).

Better Than Walking

by John H. Ackerman

The first horsecar broke the straitjacket that had kept American cities from growing for over two centuries

It was a cold, clear night and the masts of the ships along the wharves of the old whaling port of New Bedford, Massachusetts, were black lines against the stars. Fred Coon shivered a bit and his horse moved restlessly beside him as the two waited patiently at the foot of the steep hill that rose from the New Bedford end of the old wooden bridge linking the city to Fairhaven across the Acushnet River.

The pair did not have long to wait. Fred heard the crisp "tlot, tlot," of a team's hooves as they clattered along the planking. He picked up a heavy hook and a short length of chain in his right hand, gathered his reins and a whip in his left. As the New Bedford-bound horsecar left the bridge and rattled across the New Haven Railroad tracks, Fred and his horse went into action.

With the ease of long practice, Fred and his horse moved alongside the horsecar. Fred's horse matched his pace to his straining mates on the car. Fred lifted the hook he carried and dropped it through a ringbolt on the floor of the horsecar at the end of the dasher. As Fred ran easily alongside, the three horses leaned into their work, trotted around the curve and

HORSE CARS

Two-horse teams were standard, except on steep hills.

Courtesy Alton Bailey, Old Dartmouth Historical Society

When an epidemic of horse distemper killed the animals en masse, bulls and oxen were pressed into service.

up the long hill to a welcome stop halfway to the top. A pause, and the three horses leaned into their harness again to get the laden car to the top of the long ridge that looks down on New Bedford Harbor. Fred slacked off, unhooked his horse, and walked slowly back down the long hill to the little shed-stable at the end of the bridge.

For his work with New Bedford's first horse-car line, Fred received $1.00 a day—a day that began about 8:30 in the morning and ended around 11:00 at night, with an hour-and-a-quarter off for dinner and supper. Drivers, who worked much longer hours, gloried in a salary double Fred's, $2.00 a day. But to Fred Coon, his job with the horsecar line was so satisfying, so worth the remembering, that years later he wrote about his work and the coming of the horsecar and trolley lines to New Bedford with loving care and a keen memory for details. Today, his neatly-written manuscript is carefully kept in the vaults of the Whaling Museum of the Old Dartmouth Historical Society in New Bedford.

The real test for the brand-new company came when its cars had to cross the New Haven Railroad tracks. The street railway had not got around to laying its rail between those of the New Haven. So drivers whipped up their teams and hoped the heavily-loaded cars would bump across the tracks and come down on the street railway's iron on the other side. Some cars did. Some didn't.

Fred Coon carefully described the right way to drive a horsecar. As he put it: "First after the conductor gave the usual two bells, it was necessary to prevent the horses from bolting into their collars and giving them a sore neck or shoulder. If the car was on level track, you would let off the brake and hold back on your horses . . . if on an upgrade, start your horses or, rather, they would start themselves on hearing the two bells and when the traces tighten, slack off your brake and your horses have got the car (moving).

"While the car was in motion, the brake had to be adjusted frequently according to the speed of the horses to keep the car from running onto the heels of the horses. . . ."

Fred has pauses in his narrative that capture the past with sudden sharp clarity: "The writer well remembers the old box cars in Winter standing in the Fairhaven carbarn with blankets on the horses on a cold Winter night with straw on the floor and a kerosene lamp on each end of the car. . . . Before starting the driver took off the blankets, folded them up and threw them over the dasher unless it stormed when they were laid just inside the front door on the floor. . . . When the car started and the horses were trotting along, the windows in the car which were loose would jar all the way and, in coming across the bridge (from Fairhaven to New Bedford), the driver would hang his reins over the brake and beat his hands as teamsters do. . . ."

The first regular plowing of city streets after a snowfall can be credited to the horsecar lines. Some companies did mount their car bodies on runners. But most systems tried, instead, to plow their trackage. Six horses heaved at plows weighted with stones; scrapers were slung under every car, and four instead of two horses were used to haul cars when the snow was fresh and deep.

That care is well deserved. For Fred's manuscript is really the story of how the cities broke the straitjacket that kept them from growing for more than two centuries—the straitjacket imposed upon New Bedford and every American city by the need for a man to live within walking distance of his work. Trains and steamboats, even then, could bear a man swiftly across a continent or a sea. But transportation from his house to his job there was not, unless he was one of the lucky few to own a horse and carriage. Because a man had to live near his work, the three-decker tenements clustered close to high, narrow brick mills, lining streets that only saw the sun at noon.

That first horsecar enabled even a poor man to live farther away from his job. For the first

Courtesy Old Dartmouth Historical Society

Above: *The first horse car, No. 1 — of the New Bedford and Fairhaven St. Railway got rolling on pie-plate wheels in 1872.* **Below:** *A very rare photo, perhaps unique, showing oxen pulling a New Bedford horsecar during the 1872 epidemic of horse distemper.*

Courtesy Old Dartmouth Historical Society

99

Right: *New Bedford's first horsecars linked the old Pearl St. railroad depot to the steamboat wharves a mile south.*

Below: *Changing times — in the 1890s, electric trolleys (extreme left and right) swiftly drove the horsecars from the streets.*

Courtesy Old Dartmouth Historical Society

time, he could enjoy a house with a patch of green by the door where his children could play in safety and his wife could brighten a walk with a flower garden.

New Bedford grew quickly along the horsecar lines; like a kind of wheeled Johnny Appleseed they sowed suburban houses and whole new neighborhoods in their goings. One line was built west to a country crossroads; almost at once, a building boom began that ended in the built-up West End of New Bedford. The same pattern was repeated everywhere the horsecars ran. Dorchester, now a part of Boston, was an independent town until the horsecars began rolling through its streets and turned it into a Boston bedroom. Later, of course, the electric trolley, the bus, then the private car came along to replace the horsecar, but all three merely finished what the horsecars had begun.

Typically, the horsecars' start in New Bedford was modest—a little more than a mile of track from the old railroad depot to the steamboat wharf where steamers to Nantucket and Martha's Vineyard waited. Hardly sensational . . . but it was the first time railroad passengers bound for the island steamboats were given a chance to ride to the docks. A carriage ride too expensive for many of them or a one-mile walk had been their only choice before the horsecars.

Disaster struck, however, almost at once. An epidemic of horse distemper killed the animals *en masse*, including those of the new company, and left surviving animals too weak to work. Bulls and oxen were pressed into service, some in yokes, others with traditional horse harness minus the bridle. But the big beasts were slow and the city cobblestones hurt their feet, and it was with a sigh of relief that the line went back to horses a month later when the epidemic had run its course.

Early days for horsecar lines were marked by informality, Fred Coon recalls. Hungry for passengers, the Acushnet Line rushed to have its facilities ready for circus day when huge crowds could be expected to swell company coffers. Unfortunately, the new company was a trifle short of horses. A coal and wood dealer who— luckily—was one of the bigger stockholders loaned his teams for the day. But the starting bell's two rings meant nothing to the coal horses and drivers had to lead them along.

The use of extra horses suggests one truth basic to all horsecar systems: they took very good care of their horses, not because they shared the views of modern lovers of the horse, but for the same reason today's bus companies maintain their vehicles' engines with loving care. Horsecar lines had spacious and clean stables with special stalls for ailing animals. The horses were well-fed and much thought was given to their diets. Hours of work for the horses were about half those of the men. Extra horses on hills or on snow made certain the animals would not be overworked. Their training was sound, on a par with that of fire horses, or the milkman's steed that knew the route as well as his master.

The horsecar line and the city grew together. When electrification neared, the Union Street Railway was running 74 cars over 16 miles of track with 121 men and 220 horses. But the day of the horsecar in New Bedford and elsewhere came to an end early in the 1890s, not long after a brilliant engineer named Frank Sprague designed, built, and operated the first successful, practical electric trolley line in Richmond, Virginia. Success of the Virginia line doomed the horses. Conversion was quick, sometimes too quick; equipped with electric motors, many horsecars proved unequal to the new strains. Cars designed for electric operation quickly were added by system after system.

The new, swifter electric cars overstepped the city boundaries as the slower horsecars could not. New suburbs covered former farms; quiet villages that had changed little since the battles of Lexington and Concord suddenly found themselves bedroom towns. For 30 years and more, the trolley pumped more and more people from city cores to suburban fringes. Private cars and buses continued the process. The suburbs grew of their own accord to the point where now dwellers there complain bitterly of their travail in getting to and from work in the city they long ago fled. Rapid-transit trains, turbine trains, supersonic trains in tubes, monorails, and buses operating on private roads have all been suggested as remedies to the problem born with the horsecars a century or so ago.

END

LUXURY YACHTS

A Golden Era
by Manley H. Grant

Photos courtesy Bath Iron Works Corp.

The Grand Old Days before taxes and the Great Depression, when the Bath Iron Works turned out floating palaces for American millionaires at close to a million apiece...

Most of the big yachts are gone now, but they were fascinating while they lasted. The decline started with the stock market crash in the '20s.

Many stories have been written about the luxury yachts, describing them as floating palaces and toys of the rich. It was indeed a golden era for some. A man's wealth and prestige were often judged by the size of his yacht.

But there is another side to the coin which should be mentioned. At a time when jobs were scarce in our state (Maine), hundreds of men all along the coast shipped out as crewmen aboard the big yachts. Their ability as sailors and their willingness to work were well known. There were few yachts that didn't have some downeasters in the crew.

Thousands more were employed in shipyards such as the Bath Iron Works, where some of the most beautiful yachts ever built were launched.

The old Bath Iron Works closed in 1925 and all the tools and equipment were sold at auction. In 1927, the world-famous yard was taken over by the New England Public Service Company. The company planned to scuttle the yard and to use the old machine shop for making pie plates. A stream of little pie plates would be coming from the launching ways of a plant that had created some of the most efficient ships that a nation had ever built.

The situation seemed hopeless, but fortunately for Bath a native son, Pete Newell, Sr., came forward, and after many months of dickering and borrowing what money he could, reopened the yard for shipbuilding in 1928. Newell was able to assemble a crew of men who knew their craft.

In the decade of the 1920s when a surge of post-war prosperity swept over the nation, a demand arose among wealthy men for fine private yachts, finer and larger than at any time in the past. The Bath Iron Works saw the possibilities and went all out for contracts. They wanted to prove that they could build just as fine yachts as were being built in Germany or elsewhere.

The first big contract was for the yacht *Vanda* to be built for Ernest B. Dane. She would be 240' long and 36' wide. The $750,000 beauty was said to be the most luxurious yacht ever built in the United States.

As a passenger on the Mount Desert Island steamer, *Rangeley*, Dane had been struck by the high quality of the joiner work in the cabin.

"Who built that steamer?" he asked.

"Bath Iron Works, of course," Pete Newell replied.

That did it. Dane promised to advance 15% of the *Vanda*'s cost, and there was the working capital to begin on. Gielow, Inc., which had the design contract, borrowed $200,000 from the Harriman National Bank and loaned it to the Bath Iron Works. Newell returned half of it with the comment, "If I had the $200,000, we might be tempted to spend it foolishly."

According to the author Nathaniel J. Hasenfus, "It was a great day for Bath when the *Vanda* slid down the ways. On that day, if ever, Bath was in a holiday spirit." People knew that the contracts would provide a big boost to the economy of the shipbuilding city as well as the surrounding area. They had been through a period of lean years, ending with the closing of the shipyard in 1925.

America's Cup defender Ranger — *"supreme example of a J-class sloop, the highest expression of yacht-building art."*

Vanda, first private yacht to be built by the Bath Iron Works, was considered the moxt luxurious ever built in the United States.

Two other big yachts were under construction on adjacent ways. One was the *Hi Esmaro*, a twin screw, 266' dream boat being built for H. Edward Manville, the asbestos king. Cost of the *Hi Esmaro* ran close to $1,000,000. She came to a gallant end when, converted into a torpedo boat tender in World War II, she fell victim to Jap bombs somewhere east of Cape Surville on San Cristobal Island.

The second yacht was the *Paragon*, built for J. H. Davol. She was smaller, but she had her distinctive points. She bore the name of a once famous New England clipper ship whose skipper was the grandfather of *Paragon's* owner. Her modified fisherman's hull and destroyer-type superstructure set her apart from other yachts.

The diesel yacht *Caroline* was second in size to only the *Corsair*. The 279' yacht was built for Eldridge H. Johnson, former president of Victor Talking Machine Company. She had one of the largest gyroscopic stabilizers ever built. It weighed 105,000 pounds, making the ship practically rollproof in heavy seas.

On April 10, 1930, shortly after the stock market crash that ushered in the Great Depression, Bath Iron Works turned out "the cream of the crop," the incomparable *Corsair IV*, (343' long, displaced 1938 tons) for J. P. Morgan II who, like his father, could appreciate the lines and qualities of a fine ship.

While the *Corsair* was being built, Mr. Morgan spent a week in Bath. He visited the yard daily to check on the progress of construction. One of the men who worked on the *Corsair* said, "Mr. Morgan was a fine man. He never threw his weight around and he was always ready to listen to suggestions."

Residents of Bath recall that two private Pullmans brought Morgan and his party to Bath over the Maine Central tracks, and on to the siding at the plant. The financier gave notice that he wanted no publicity. So the yard was closed to the public for the launching. Maine ingenuity asserted itself, however. There was the new Carleton Bridge only a few hundred yards away from which spectators had a wonderful view of the proceedings. An enterprising lady who lived near the shipyard rented a window to people who wanted to take snapshots. She charged $5.00 apiece for the window privilege.

After the sea trials over the course at Rockland, Morgan told B.I.W. president Pete Newell,

"I am completely satisfied with her."

"There are some things that don't quite satisfy me," Newell said. "I think we had better go back to Bath to make a few adjustments and finishing touches."

"She suits me just the way she is," Morgan replied. "Let's go for New York."

The Morgans used the *Corsair* for several years as a private yacht, but in May, 1940, shortly after the beginning of World War II, Morgan turned the ship over to the British Admiralty. She served on patrol duty throughout the war, based in Bermuda. After the war she was returned to the Morgans and was converted into a commercial cruise ship on the west coast. In 1948, she stranded near Acapulco, Mexico and was abandoned as a total loss.

The steel express yacht *Winchester*, built for W. P. Rouse, was unique in design. She was built for speed, 31.55 knots, and had a destroyer hull to achieve it. For years the *Winchester* commuted between Newport and New York City in less time than you could take the trip by train. This writer saw the *Winchester* many times on Long Island Sound. She passed the other yachts as if they were anchored.

The last steam yacht to be launched in 1930 was the *Aras*, for Hugh J. Chisholm of Portland, Maine, and New York City. Chisholm was head of the Oxford Paper Company. The *Aras* was 243′ and displaced 1294 tons. She was larger than Chisholm's first *Aras*, which was built by the old Bath Iron Works Ltd. in 1924. After her service in World War II, she became the presidential yacht *Williamsburg*. Presidents Eisenhower and Truman used her frequently.

At the time of the *Aras* launching in 1930, 1032 men were busy at the Iron Works, compared with the 300 men who worked in the plant when the *Vanda* was built in 1927.

Other big yachts were built after 1930, but the stock market crash of 1929 presaged the end of the era for the big private yachts. Only a few hardy yachtsmen had the courage or the money to operate such craft during the depression years.

The end of the epoch nearly wrote finis to the Bath Iron Works for the second time. The bottom had really dropped out of the yacht-building business. The company was stuck with one of the 190-footers built on speculation with an investment of $50,000.

Sailing yachts, large and small, have played a prominent part in the history of American yachting. Any sailing yacht over 65′ can be put into the category of really large yachts.

The most famous sailing yacht built at Bath Iron Works was the America's Cup defender *Ranger*, built for Harold Vanderbilt. The internationally-known yachtsman had skippered the *Enterprise* to victory in 1930.

Yachtsmen agree that Vanderbilt's superior skill as a skipper was responsible for the victory. A crewman on the challenging English yacht claimed that Vanderbilt had used unfair tactics such as "stealing the English yacht's wind." This is a perfectly legal tactic in racing, however. When sailing beside an opponent, a good skipper can maneuver his boat so that his sails take the wind away from the other yacht, thus gaining a temporary advantage.

In 1934, Vanderbilt was again victorious with the *Rainbow* in a very close contest with T.O.M. Sopwith's *Endeavor I*. Knowledgeable yachtsmen of the day held the opinion that, all things being equal, *Endeavor I* was a faster boat than *Rainbow*—indeed the fastest sailing yacht ever built.

When a new challenge came from Sopwith and a new *Endeavor*, it was believed that the *Rainbow* would surely lose to *Endeavor II*, which was likely to be an even faster boat than Sopwith's first great sloop. Vanderbilt realized that if he were to meet the challenge successfully, he would need a new and faster boat.

When the challenge came in 1936, Vanderbilt and the flag officers at the New York Yacht Club appointed W. Starling Burgess and Olin J. Stevens to jointly design the prospective cup defender.

Vanderbilt had already held preliminary negotiations with the Bath Iron Works to build the racer, and now he came down to Bath in a gloomy mood.

"Looks as though I'll have to meet the challenge with the *Rainbow* again," he told Pete Newell. The Cup committee had failed to come up with its share of the money, so most of the cost would have to be borne by the Vanderbilt family.

Newell said, "I don't know because I have

105

never built one like it. But you have built these boats before. What do you think it should cost?"

Vanderbilt didn't have a ready answer. He realized that the cost of labor and materials had enormously increased and a complicated calculation would be necessary to estimate the price of such a new boat.

Finally Newell said, "I'll tell you what I'll do. I will build her for cost with a ceiling of $130,000—cost of labor, cost of materials, and 50% of the labor cost for overhead."

"Do you mean hull, mast, main boom and spinnaker at cost?"

"That's right. I mean at cost," the shipbuilder replied.

Shortly after Vanderbilt returned to New York he phoned Newell to "Go ahead."

The rest of the story is history. The beautiful *Ranger* was considered the greatest of all the J-Class Cup defenders. Her brilliant successes have become an epic in yacht racing history. She made a clean sweep of her America's Cup races against *Endeavor II*. She was hailed as the supreme example of a J-Class sloop—the highest expression of yacht building art.

Garnett Laidlaw, in his book, *The Cradle of Ships*, mentions Sherman Hoyt, one of America's great sailors, who said of the *Ranger* in his memoirs, "Take her all-in-all, we shall never look upon her like again."

The *Ranger*, along with many other American yachts, made the supreme sacrifice for her country in World War II. Her huge keel was needed for the hungry furnaces of our war industries. She was broken up and melted down soon after Pearl Harbor.

The largest of all sailing yachts was built at the Germania yard in Kiel. Her overall length was 316' and she had a beam (width) of 49'. She was originally called the *Hussar*, later re-named *Sea Cloud*. Her name was finally changed to *Angelita* when she became state yacht of the Dominican Republic. Designed by Cox and Stevens, she was rigged as a four-masted barque. Her monthly running costs were reckoned at $15,000.

My introduction to yachting came in 1928

Sea trial of the first Aras *built for Hugh J. Chisholm by the Bath Iron Works — May 27, 1924.*

106

when I found a berth on the big steam yacht, *Saelmo,* owned by William Todd, the shipbuilder who eventually owned yards on the East and West Coasts as well as in South America. During World War II, the Todds were part owners of the Todd-Bath shipyard in South Portland.

The *Saelmo* was a beautiful 180′ yacht with a clipper bow. With the all-white hull and varnished deck houses, she was a sight to behold.

The *Saelmo* was essentially a private yacht used by the Todd family and their friends. But Mr. Todd's shipbuilding enterprise was big business, and many parties entertained on board the *Saelmo* were composed of American and foreign officials with whom the shipbuilder had business dealings.

As far as the crew was concerned, the days were a mixture of work, some excitement and a lot of fun. There was excitement and some suspense the day we were in collision with the ferryboat off the Statue of Liberty in New York Harbor. We had a big party of church ladies aboard and most of them were frightened indeed. Fortunately no one was hurt and neither ship was damaged below the waterline. But a piece of our bowsprit was snapped off as it raked the side of the wooden ferryboat.

A marine trial was held that winter to determine which vessel was responsible for the accident. Now a marine court is very precise, and they don't make any allowances for guesswork. When our captain was on the witness stand, the court asked him how far he was from a certain buoy when the ships came together.

"I would say about 300′," Captain Nagle responded.

"We want to know exactly and no 'abouts'," the marine official cautioned him.

Later, the captain told us he couldn't say for sure that he had given the right answer, but that's the way it has to be in a marine trial.

The verdict was decided in favor of shipbuilder Todd. Members of the crew thought it would go that way. Several minutes before the boats had collided, our captain had signalled his intentions (three times in fact) to keep on course, but there had been no response from the ferryboat.

Todd was a good friend and backer of Alfred E. Smith, Governor of New York at the time. On several occasions we picked the governor and his friends up at New York City and took them up the Hudson River to Albany.

One day when Governor Smith arrived, I was on duty at the gangway to help the passengers aboard. As soon as the governor stepped on deck he said in that familiar, rasping voice, "Where's the steward? I'm hungry." It seemed that the governor was always hungry.

In 1928, Governor Smith won his party's nomination for President with the help of his friend and associate, Franklin D. Roosevelt. "The Happy Warrior," as Roosevelt called Smith, lost the election to Herbert Hoover in a rather bitter campaign.

Mr. Todd's grandson was a frequent visitor aboard the yacht. Ironically, the boy's father, who managed one of the Todd shipyards, was a Hoover supporter. One day the young lad appeared on the *Saelmo* with his jacket covered with Hoover buttons. When Mr. Todd arrived and saw the boy, he put up quite a fuss and

"If you have to ask what a yacht costs, you can't afford one," said J.P. Morgan, who paid $2,500,000 in 1930 for the incomparable Corsair IV.

ordered him to remove the buttons—pronto!

The dapper mayor of New York City, James J. (Jimmy) Walker, and his party were frequent guests aboard the yacht. Walker, who was often referred to as "The Playboy Mayor," was always the life of the party. During dinner he usually entertained his friends with humorous stories about his life as mayor of the world's then largest city.

There was plenty of work for the crew in order to keep the yacht up to snuff. After a cruise during rough weather, the varnished cabins and rails were covered with salt spray. If it were left on too long, it could ruin the varnish, so we would have to clean all the woodwork with fresh water. Salt water discolors the brass, which also had to be scrubbed and polished.

It wasn't all work though, and there were many interesting things to remember. After the collision with the ferryboat, we needed a few repairs and were towed to the Tebo Yacht Basin, one of the Todd shipyards in Brooklyn. The crew didn't mind because it meant a chance to take in some good shows at the Brooklyn Paramount Theater where Rudy Vallee was the big attraction, or an evening at Coney Island Amusement Park.

After the yachting season ended, part of the crew remained to put the *Saelmo* away for winter. Furnishings were put in a storage building. The final job was to erect the deck house which would protect the yacht in winter weather. Then the crew members would return to their homes. Some would find jobs, but for others it meant standing by until the next yachting season rolled around. END

Hi Esmaro, 266-foot dream boat of asbestos king H. Edward Manville, was destroyed by Japanese bombs during World War II.

The Philosopher's Animal
by Norman Myrick

"... a good driver with a well broken yoke needs nothing but his voice and his brains to handle a pair of cattle."

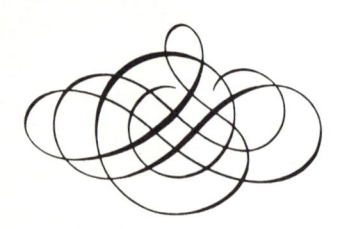

OXEN

An ox is a philosopher's animal. What he thinks he can do he will do. What he thinks he cannot do he will not do and all the king's horses and all the king's men cannot alter his mind once it is made up. Indeed, the difference between a good ox and a poor one is so much a matter of the mind that ox drivers, while they may not assume the physical characteristics of their cattle, certainly learn to see problems from the ox point of view. As Jim Avery from up in Buckland used to say when he was developing his world champion yoke, "The Lord made 'em capable, we've got to make 'em willin'."

There was a time not all that many years ago when oxen were the chief draft animal on the farm. It was the custom in Wilmington, Vermont, when Cattle Show time arrived to divide the town in half and see which section could muster the longest ox train. Yokes of oxen hitched nose to tail stretching away for a quarter of a mile were not uncommon achievements. And the universality of the animal in an earlier era is reflected in the words of Yankee Doodle when he evaluated the weight of one of General Washington's cannon as a "load for father's cattle."

I would like to say that the reason for the popularity of oxen among our Yankee farmers lay in the fact that they found in their cattle the counterpart to their own earthy character. There is a sort of poetic satisfaction in the idea that the master recognized in his slave the mirror of his own faults and virtues. The true reason, however, is much more in the Yankee tradition. The ox was simply the most economical source of power available. Cows were always more plentiful than horses and every bull calf was a potential ox. Furthermore the ox thrived on a diet of pasture grass and hay. He was less susceptible to disease than a horse and he was the source of fertility for the rocky fields of the hill country farms. As a clincher, when his usefulness as a draft animal was over he represented nearly a ton of first-class beef.

The terminology of the ox fraternity is a thing unto itself. Gee and Haw, meaning go right or go left, are reasonably well known, but when one gets into the niceties of an ox versus a stag or the desirability of a goad stick as opposed to a fish pole, some clarification is necessary. Oxen are male cattle that have been, as our mid-Victorian forebears described it, "altered." An animal that is operated upon when a week or two old grows up to be an ox or a steer. There are certain advantages to be gained, however, if the process is delayed until the creature is somewhat more mature. The result is called a "stag" and though the debates around the cracker barrel are endless and will doubtless continue as long as cattle

Fall ploughing.

bear the yoke, the stag is more nimble than a steer, perhaps a bit tougher and certainly less tractable. There are many stalwart souls, like Henry King who lived up on Flat Hills in Amherst, Massachusetts, who swore by and sometimes at his eternal pair of stags. But Mr. Wade of Williamsburg, an ox man of three-quarters of a century fancied steers. It is one of those arguments long since departed from the realm of logic behind the golden curtain of faith.

The mention of stags always brings to my mind the tale of Sam Wallace and the blizzard of '88. "It come on to snow," Sam said. "'n it snowed 'till a man had no reason to doubt it. Snow piled up four foot on the level n' still comin' down. There was a weddin' fixed to take place at the time 'n as luck would have it it happened to be mine. Well, t'was no weather for a horse so I yoked up my cattle n' headed 'em down the road. I hung onto their tails. Well, sir, them cattle jest laid their noses on top of the snow n' started to swim. I reckon when you stop to think about it that I'm the only man in the world was ever drug to his weddin' hanging onto the tails of a pair o' stags."

According to Earl Purrington of Buckland, one of the best drivers in the business, a good driver with a well broken yoke needs nothing but his voice and his brains in order to handle a pair of cattle. Most oxmen and their teams fail to reach this happy state and it is customary for the driver to carry some kind of whip. There is a definite geographical pattern governing the type of instrument used. State of Mainers use a stick, four or five feet long, with a brad protruding from one end. This is the true goad unchanged since the days of Abraham. Do not call it a goad, however, at least in the presence of a downeaster, any more than you would call a boat a boat. If you aspire to a grade above greenhorn along the Androscoggin and the Penobscot you will call it a "go-ud stick."

Massachusetts men use a short hickory switch bearing a thin rawhide lash. The whipstock is made by taking a hickory withe and sawing it lengthwise so that there are four quarters emanating from the handle. These quarters are inserted in holes bored in a piece of timber and as the whip is withdrawn they are twisted into a tough, limber braid. State of Mainers see little virtue in a braided hickory whip and Bay Staters see approximately the same amount of logic in the "go-ud stick." Both schools, however, are united in their low opinion of the elongated saplings employed by their colleagues from Connecticut and refer to them with a noble contempt as "fish poles." I suppose that what this local difference really represents is a residue of the colonial provincialism which Kenneth Roberts described so magnificently in his stories on the Revolution.

Draft cattle are designated as the nigh ox and the off ox. The driver always takes up a position at the shoulder of the left-hand ox which thereby

"... them cattle jest laid their noses on top of the snow n' started to swim."

Bringing in the sap.

becomes the nearest or nigh ox, the other animal, of course, becomes the off ox. The driver's position and the designation of the cattle is another custom of ancient lineage that has come down unchanged through countless generations.

There are a host of other terms in the ox driver's vocabulary that give it a patina of distinction. When the use of a whip is indicated a driver will "touch up" a horse, but he "hoes down" an ox. If the yoke fits snugly to the neck, it is "bowed up." A calf that has been made into an ox has been "cut," and though oxen may move five tons of stone on a straight drag they never pull a pound; they "draw." There is a nice point of grammar involved here. An ox driver will tell you how much his cattle can draw or how much they have "drawed," but he steadfastly refuses to recognize "drew" or "drawn" as good usage.

A peculiar facet of the Yankee character is reflected in the ox driver. Psychologists might diagnose the phenomenon as some form of emotional release or perhaps some hunger for self-expression. Whatever the explanation, some of the most celebrated hill country characters made their reputations with their cattle. Old Nate Cote for years drove up to the Danbury Connecticut Fair with fifteen cattle hitched to his antiquated surry led by an ancient black horse. Nate was something of an originator. He had a set of harness made for his oxen and dressed them up in gear designed for horses complete with collars. Up in Maine at the Skowhegan Fair a farmer comes each year driving an ox, resplendent in a Hereford's red and white, hitched to a venerable buggy. There never was a more perfect example of sly Yankee humor than the sedate parade the pair make each year around the race track. One is never quite sure who is laughing at who, whether the people are laughing at the grotesque rig on the track or whether the ox and his driver are laughing at the spectators.

Not long ago a teamster brought his cattle into the drawing pit at the Danbury Fair. He was having a rugged time with John Barleycorn with the decision obviously going to John. Officials attempted to dissuade him from drawing, but he was there and he was going to draw. He could scarcely stand alone and hung onto the horn of the nigh ox for support. How he ever hooked on will remain one of those unfathomable occurrences that belong somewhere between miracle and fantasy. Hook on he did and then lurching up to the security of the nigh ox he took off his cap and threw it down on the ground two feet in front of his team. "There," he said to his cattle. "Want you should draw up to there. Now git." Why they did it or how they did it will never be known, but they did it. Lifted their great shoulders into the yoke, moved up to the cap and stopped. Up to the cap the man had said and up to the cap they would go, that far and no farther.

Above: *Woodstock, Vermont. Farmer Eldridge poses with his sons on their ox cart.* **Below:** *"the black team" — a handsomely matched pair.*

114

Jim Avery of Buckland was the greatest showman of them all. Around the turn of the century he developed a yoke of Holsteins that grew into champions. They were Mack and Jerry, huge cattle that stood six feet at the shoulder. For years they were the best draft cattle in New England and probably the world. At Brattleboro they drew 11,200 pounds on a stone boat to establish a world's record. Mr. Avery realized that he had an exceptional team and when their best draft days were over he proceeded to feed them up until they became "the largest cattle in the world." A special tent was made for the oxen in which Mr. Avery showed them throughout the nation. The picture of Jim's son sitting on a rocking chair up on Mack's broad back was the pin-up picture of the day. When Mack went the way of all oxen he tipped the scales at 4700 pounds. The butcher who closed Mack's career advertised steaks from "the largest ox in the world." He disposed of 37 other carcasses in Mack's name before the sale was over. Mack wasn't fat. He didn't waddle. He was simply huge. If you happen to be passing through Shelburne Falls in Massachusetts drop in at Sid Wood's office by the livery stable and take a look at Mack's famous picture. If you get over Buckland way stop in at Earl Purrington's store. There is a picture of Mack and Jerry hanging up behind the counter. Earl used to drive them years ago. He was there when they set the record at Brattleboro, a record that he broke years later with another pair of Holsteins. "They was champions," Earl says, "they drawed on whatever ground the good Lord provided. If they was to draw today on them special pits they give us at the fairs they ain't nothin' could stop them. Nothin'."

One hardly thinks of applying the word "gallant" to oxen. They may be wise, they may be patient, but hardly gallant. Go to the drawing pits then, my friend. Go to the drawing pits when the leaves begin to turn and fair-time spills over the land. You'll see them there, the oxen and the drivers, each chewing their respective cuds. The old-timers, grizzled and bent, with their beards and their memories, the middle-aged farmers convinced that this year they have a winner, the sons and the grandsons each with a whip or a go-ud stick or fish-pole marking his geographical origin. The great cattle swing into the ring with yokes creaking, chains jingling. Watch the driver hook on. Notice how he hitches as close to the "boat" as he can and still have clearance for his cattle. He stands back now and looks the team over. That nigh ox, the driver hitches him two inches closer to his mate. The right hind foot of the off ox needs to come up a hair, the driver taps the hoof with his whip and makes the adjustment. They are standing well now, ready to lift into the yoke when he gives the word. With something akin to a caress they take up the slack in the chain. It is part of the ritual, part of that tense moment of expectancy when man and beasts stand poised for that one mighty instant when flesh and blood are turned to the task. Then—"Git up you black-hearted sons o' satan. Hi-hi-hi-hi-hi-hi-hi." Two thundering bodies boring into the yoke, heads up, shoulders lifting, steel-shod hooves churning the red clay in a turbulent pattern of power. Yes it moves. Two feet in Connecticut, six feet in Massachusetts, as far as you can go in Maine. It makes no difference for the end is the same. A driver mopping his brow with a red bandana. A pair of cattle standing under the yoke, their flanks heaving like a blacksmith's bellows, and over the public address system come the golden words, "It's a draw, Mr. Guildford, an up an' down honest to God draw and ninety eight hundred on the boat."

That is all there is to it. Two oxen and a man moving five tons of stone on a straight draw. No pari-mutuels, no colored silks and dazzling prima donnas, two oxen and a man. And so you get into your car, with your fluid drive and your sixty horses. You get into your car and drive home through the purple autumn twilight. Perhaps you chuckle at the thought of Nate Cote and his outlandish train of cattle. Perhaps you grow indignant at the recollection of a slashing whip when some over zealous driver "hoed down" his cattle in public. Again it doesn't matter because this day you saw an art as ancient as history unfolded in the drawing pit. As it was with Genghis Khan and the Caesars, as it was with the Chaldeans and the Pharaohs of the Nile, so it was today. Two oxen and a man, strange ponderous creatures plodding their inexorable way across the centuries. The sloe-eyed ox, Homer called them, gallant beasts of burden that have marked the course of empire. END

That You Mabel?
by Haydn S. Pearson

That's the way Father began every telephone call. He stepped up to the box on the kitchen wall, gave a determined long ring, and when she asked, "Number please?" Father said, "That you, Mabel?"

Then he'd likely say, "If Bert Adams is home, I'd talk with him a minute."

Father never gave his name. He didn't need to, for Mabel knew every voice in town. She also knew whether Bert was home, or whether he had gone over to Peterborough, and if so, about what time he would be home.

In the days when a man could turn a crank and get Central, instead of pushing a calloused finger into a doo-dinky little hole and swinging the jointless contraption around half a dozen times, Central knew all that was going on, and she used judgment in what she reported.

Half a century ago, Mabel was the town's focal point of information and she was allowed to tell you the news. At exactly high noon, she gave one long ring and everyone in town listened while she read the weather report from the daily paper and perhaps gave a headline or two.

In the days of rural free delivery by horse and buggy, half the town didn't get its mail until well into the afternoon. We all knew Mabel would ring at exactly twelve and so no one used the telephone for a minute or two before twelve until after she called.

It was always interesting when I called Eddie, my friend a mile up the road, to hear the receivers come down. Then as soon as Eddie answered, you could hear the receivers click back on the two-pronged hooks. The conversation of a couple of 12-year-olds wasn't interesting.

It was one summer vacation that the event occurred about which I still wonder. Mother had been trying to get Mrs. Adams up the road to come down for a visit. But as usual, Mrs. Smith, as we'll call her, was on the line.

Mrs. Smith was famous as a long-winded talker. She was a dear old soul, living out the sunset years with her son's family. When Mrs. Smith got on the line with a phone pal, she was good for half an hour or more. We all liked

CRANK 'PHONES

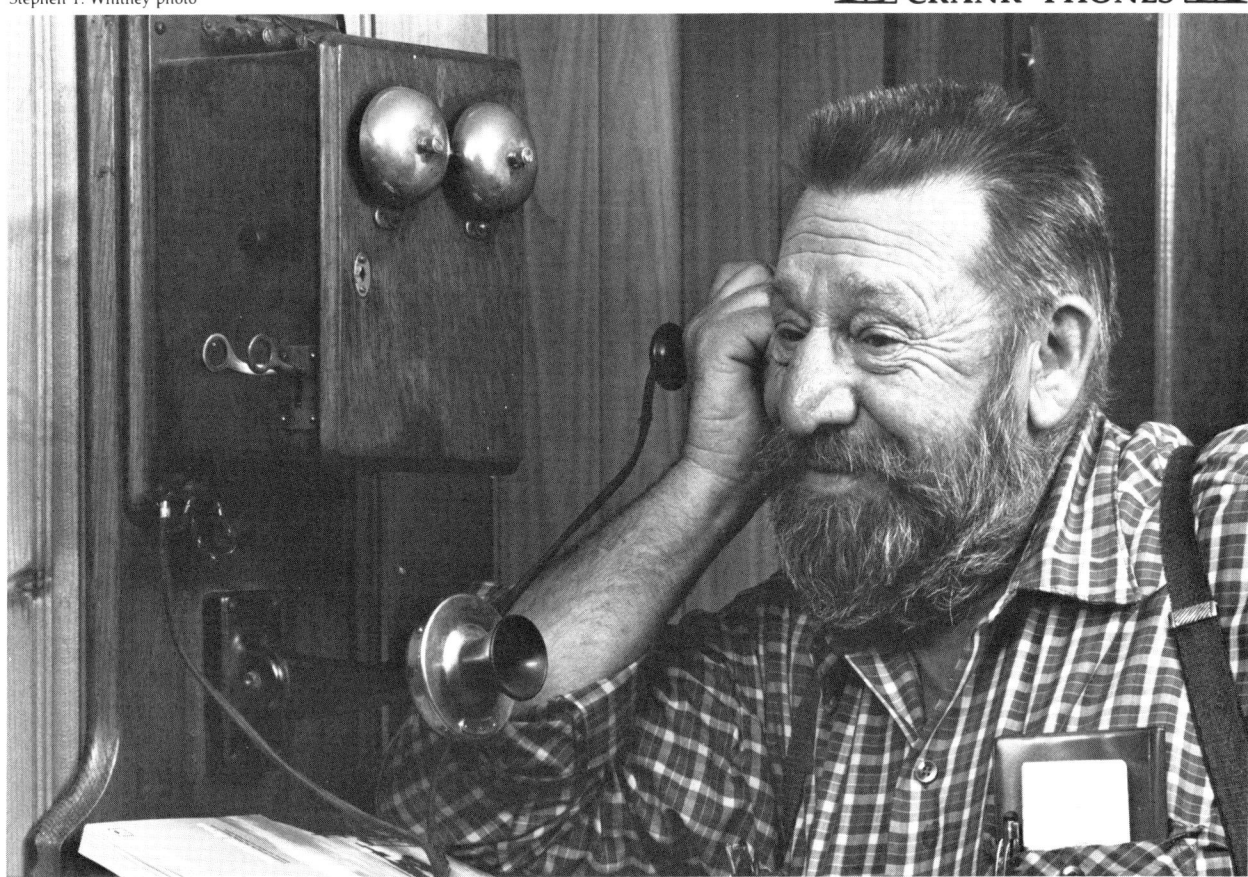

Grammie Smith, but we all complained of her telephone calls.

I was home from college and feeling my oats. "I'll fix her," I said to Mother. "You don't have to take this sort of treatment."

"No, don't trouble her," Mother answered. "The poor soul needs the telephone. Still I wish she would hang up."

"I'll fix her," I repeated. I remember Father, resting on the kitchen sofa, opened an eye and smiled. Sister Edith said, "Go ahead. She needs a lesson."

So I walked over to the phone. I took off the receiver, and with my shoulder jammed the hook down so I couldn't be heard.

Then I made a speech. "Mrs. Smith," I said, "this is Haydn Pearson, the minister's son, and I am speaking for my mother and the whole town. You are monopolizing the telephone. You are inconveniencing all the subscribers on this line. In plain English, you are very selfish."

I thought Mother would faint until Edith walked over and whispered in her ear. I went on for a few minutes and then hung up. "There," I said. "That'll fix her. You won't have any trouble from now on."

It is about forty years since that afternoon. And I still wonder. I would swear I had pressed the hook down so I couldn't be heard. But the fact stands. After that day, Mrs. Smith rarely talked over ten minutes.

Just the other day I read that soon I shall be able to jab my finger into that small hole and dial a number to get a response across the nation. Probably it is progress.

But just once more I would like to step up to that plain brown box between the kitchen windows, turn the crank and hear Mabel say "Number please?"

Then I'd ask Mabel how she was and if she knew whether Bill Hanson had gone to Peterborough with his father. Mabel would tell me, and then ask me to tell Mother that Mrs. Hanson was going to call her as soon as she finished baking a three-layer chocolate cake for the Ladies Sewing Circle dinner. *That* was telephone service.

END

The "Yard" *by Florence B. Jacobs*

Great-aunt Martha's mock-orange scented the farthest corner; small cinnamon roses, run wild, banked a slope; Gram's lemon lilies spread out into the abutting hayfield.

We didn't call it the *churchyard*, because it never was.

A white steeple tops the north hill, there is a dip into and through the village, and The Yard snuggles just under the south hill, so near that sounds of small-town life flow over those who are still a part.

We didn't use the more formal *cemetery*, either, nor a plain, stern Pilgrim *burying-ground*. Graveyard was softened to The Yard, an extension of that at home. And from childhood, The Yard has had as familiar a place in my background.

A gentle green slope curving down to the little cove with its harbor. Millstream draining over a dam at the end. Three giant pines for a gate. The quiet accented by cascading water and young voices merged to the quality of bird song. . . . Sobering of course, thought-provoking; but not frightening, not grim.

Mother's favorite summer-afternoon pastime was to meet a friend there. After pulling chickweed and scouring lichens from century-old stones with good strong soda water, they would rest on the cement curbing around Great-aunt Ca'line's lot for a little gossip, flavored with warm, tender, sometimes dramatic reminiscence. . . .

Of Aunt Ca'line's beloved only daughter, who rode the six miles from Skowhegan through a northeast blizzard in ball gown and shawl, and died of pneumonia within the week— miles we now do casually and cozily even in January. . . .

Of Mother's "reserved" bachelor cousin who gave me the gold watch the summer I was

DECORATION DAY

eighteen, graduated from high and ready to teach grade school here in September. He must have been waiting that morning in his house next door, have cut across to intercept me as I started down the path. "Here," he said, eyes straight ahead, thrusting into my hand the shiny new hunter case and the long flexible chain which had been his mother's. "Going to be a schoolmarm, you'll need a timepiece." He was gone, taking long strides. And I had never before been sure he knew I was alive! . . .

My special friend and I, passing in bathing suits on our way to the lake, might spend a twilit hour on that same curbing, the hilarity bubbling through most of our conversations subdued only a little.

Since nearly every local family owned at least one lot, caring for these was a definite community project, though not organized as such. During three seasons we bore flowers for a Saturday bedecking. The lilacs growing beside any village doorstep; blush roses from the bush under dining-room windows; heliotrope; later mauve, white or coral sweet peas and velvety pansies; orange-into-copper nasturtiums; *late, late* asters and heavy-headed dahlias. Autumn leaves pinned with their own stems into a garland; sprays of evergreen and cones to last out the white winter.

If time pressed or posies lacked, it didn't matter, their own grew richly about them. Great-aunt Martha's mock-orange scented the farthest corner; small cinnamon roses, run wild, banked a slope; Gram's lemon lilies spread out into the abutting hayfield. Scarlet geraniums such as she coddled year long were set out around our granite monument. And it was a family joke that Mother always urged someone to go water these before it rained!

Every few weeks lawn mowers had to be trundled along, sometimes scythes, and sickles for hand trimming. Trespassing alders were yanked out to let valley lilies take over. No lot was neglected; each family "saw to" its own, whether third cousins twice-removed or stepdaughter of a distant uncle.

For the town plot which held a few nameless tramps like the so-called Tommy Slambang, people clubbed together, as they did for the double stone under which lie twin brothers who came from the urban dangers of Chicago and drowned swimming in a placid country millpond. . . . I remember lining their grave with boughs. Home from a Skowhegan office and prowling as usual down the shore, I found old Mr. Wakefield, the sexton, fretting as he dug. "Newturned earth looks so *raw*," he said, "but I'm too lame, now, to climb down in." So of course, like the little red hen, *I* did.

Even the single grave outside (whose strong-willed occupant had vowed he'd never lie within the disputed fence, under the disapproved slab) was cleared of hawkweed and its teetering marker righted.

The highlight, the climax, of this painstaking care came at Memorial time, then called Decoration Day and *observed* rather than *celebrated*. It was kept almost as a religious festival, a flowery spring rite like those of ancient Brittany. The whole previous afternoon was given to last preparations. We scouted orchards for ungrafted apple trees bearing sour fruit but ineffable shell-pink blossoms—for armfuls of greenish-white bird cherry, even late shadbush.

Some felt that "boughten" flowers, costing more, proved greater respect and love. Others held that offerings must be homegrown, nurtured with long patience. . . . I am always somehow sure that Mother will prize jonquils picked beside our own stone wall.

Supper was sketchy—hulled corn and yellow-flecked milk, dandelion greens warmed over, fritters with new maple syrup—and the dishes quickly done. Baskets saved from family funerals were brought down from the attic chamber; Great-aunt Ann's for her; Grandpa's, never forgetting this must hold tulips of his favorite dark crimson. These we would range on the attic stairs and build up from the great pails of gathered blossoms. Lay a good solid base of dogwood or cherry boughs. Then, careful stalk by single spray, set tulip, narcissus, lilac, to best advantage. Stand back, head cocked at an angle, criticize or admire.

Next morning pile loose flowers into the wicker basket which could hold a week's washing; stack individual containers in the back seat. Swallow a hasty cup of coffee . . . hurry, *hurry* to be first in The Yard. This was a matter of face, of prestige, along with friendly rivalry over who had the most bouquets, most tastefully arranged.

Once all tributes were in place, one could stroll at ease, a hostess greeting late comers, friends not seen since last May, returned from distant cities or even another coast. Visit in small, low-voiced groups, slapping away black flies and midges but not giving ground.

Make a final circuit to assure ourselves that no lot outdoes ours; another trip to the lake for water to replenish all vases; pull one black tulip up to show and snip off a snapdragon already withered.

Just before noon start home again to the slighted household chores with a sense of reunion in a sunlit place, of fellowship and enduring peace. Even after a committal—even when we turned back without a beloved uncle —it wasn't leaving him behind, alone, but literally gathered to his fathers.

In a single lot reaching from aisle to aisle, lie Grandfather George and Grandmother Ann, his father Lucius and mother Sally, all four of *their* parents, Gideon and Martha Lincoln,

Robert and Mary Morrison. A few steps away are Gram's parents, David and Susan McLaughlin; the brother who drowned as a boy; the one who lived to be old—with eyes clear and blue as a child's.

The Lincoln generation before that lies in a cemetery three miles north, and three miles south, near the upper line of the Plymouth Claim, rest McLaughlin forebears. Both of these cemeteries antedate the village.

Mother had a Scottish feeling for these bonds. And as an offshoot, loved to explore tangled overgrown plots on deserted farms, their leaning slabs of slate with weeping willows rampant; to decipher inscriptions on more affluent marble blocks, *f*'s for *s*'s, carved lambs and cherubs.

Sunday afternoon drives often led to, but not always by, such cemeteries. I have a mental color shot of her in one near Chesterville, coming down aisles flooded with sunshine and hedged by tall pines, wearing a light summer voile, a radiant smile . . . she had found an old family lot with a completely new ancestor!

And if all this seems a little like a cult of ancestor worship, it still wasn't a bad heritage for a child, that sense of continuity and close ties, of tradition, of stable values that can keep a heart from restless drifting.   END

Magic on Main Street

All photographs for this chapter are courtesy the Redpath Chautauqua Collection, Special Collections Department, University of Iowa Libraries.

CHAUTAUQUAS

by Albert G. Miller

The great Chautauqua Movement was "the most American thing in America" — a feast of oratory, music and entertainment.

When a certain small boy of the early 1920's heard that a politician distinguished for his oratory was coming to town with a tent Chautauqua, he was greatly perplexed. "Pop," he asked, "what is oratory, anyway?"

"Well," came the thoughtful reply, "if a public speaker tells you that black is white, that's just plain silly. But if he tells you that black is white, gets red in the face, bellows like a bull and pounds the table with his fists—son, that's *oratory!*"

While that explanation may seem oversimplified, it accurately described the flamboyant variety of speechmaking that stirred the blood of rural American audiences during the first quarter of this century. For it was the orator—the trumpet-voiced spellbinder, roaring and pounding his message home—who constituted the backbone of the tent Chautauqua circuits.

The great Chautauqua Movement, which reached its zenith in 1924, was called by Theodore Roosevelt "the most American thing in America." Rooted in religion and respectability, the Chautauqua took to the road in 1903, selling "culture" for cash to 30 million people in 12,000 communities along the circuits. Without radio, television or talking pictures to provide the mental stimulation they sought, the citizens welcomed the annual Chautauqua Week.

With few exceptions, every well known speechmaker of the era uncovered veins of gold on the summer circuits. Their "inspirational" lectures were referred to by the managers (off the record) as "Mother, Home and Heaven" numbers. And William Jennings Bryan—the Silver-Tongued Orator, the Old Dependable, the Greatest of Them All—was the most popular Mother, Home and Heavener who ever traveled the Chautauqua road.

Although Bryan was the darling of the Brown Tent set, there were some big-city scoffers who

Sam Jones, the famous evangelist, described the Chautauqua as "a cross between a camp meeting and a county fair."

The ideal program was one part lecture and two parts variety, dramatics, and music of every conceivable kind.

belittled his methods and messages. Indeed, some disdainful jokers borrowed a quip that had been going the rounds and applied it to Bryan himself. Two men, as the story went, are discussing after-dinner speakers. "Take Bryan," says one of them, "he's a most unusual man. Just put a dinner in his mouth and out comes a speech." "Right," says the other. "And just put a speech in his mouth and out comes your dinner."

To the dwellers in the hinterland, "going to Chautauqua" meant sitting down to a week's feast of rhetoric and entertainment, served twice daily inside the big brown tent. To the "talent" —preachers, politicians, performers, authors and assorted celebrities—it meant extra income during an otherwise unprofitable summer season.

On the days when the headliners were scheduled to appear, special trainloads of ticket holders arrived on the sidings, while the roads into town were choked with farm wagons and Model T's. It was said that Bryan was good for 40 acres of parked Fords anywhere he went. That eloquent sermonizer, with his indestructible, cast-iron voice, followed the Chautauqua trails season after season, and his drawing power never decreased.

While Bryan's most popular lecture was "The Prince of Peace," he often prefaced his religious message with a few thousand fiery words about Prohibition, which, it goes without saying, he championed with all his heart, soul and lungs. In one town, where the chief industry was the brewing of schnapps, Bryan attacked the Demon Rum with such eloquence that even the brewers themselves leaped to their feet and almost resolved to sign the pledge. *Almost,* that is, for they regained their senses in a hurry after Bryan left town.

It was estimated at the time that Bryan had spoken to more people, face to face, than any other man in history. That evaluation is conceivable, for Bryan appeared on 3000 Chautauqua platforms. A man of immense vigor, he never seemed to grow weary of the killing pace and never complained, even of the heat which kept him constantly damp. His trademark was a palm-leaf fan, with which he stirred up the stifling air of the prairies. At every appearance he insisted upon having a large block of ice resting in a pan beside him on the speakers' table. While orating, he rested one hand on the ice, and when his bare pate became lobster-red he transferred the frigid palm to his scalp. Numerous witnesses have sworn that upon those occasions they actually saw steam rising from Bryan's head.

Another story concerning one of the Mother, Home and Heaveners is related by Gay MacLaren, an actress who traveled the circuits for many years. In her colorful volume of Chautauqua reminiscences, *Morally We Roll Along,* Miss MacLaren tells of one "sob speaker" who described, with gestures, how a tiny girl with golden curls expired and was taken by the Lord to join the angels, clutching a puppy in her cold, chubby arms. The speaker then gazed upward with tear-filled eyes and bleated, "Oh, God, why didn't you take me instead of the child?" Instantly there came an answer from the rear of the tent: "It's not too late, God. Do it now!"

Regardless of minority opinions, the Chautauqua orators flourished and grew even more popular as the years went by. Robert M. La Follette, the political leader from Wisconsin, thundered his progressive ideas from the tent platforms, cooling his overworked throat with frequent draughts of ice water. "Fighting Bob" was known to Chautauqua audiences as a "four-pitcher" man, which automatically made him a true colossus of oratory, for even Bryan consumed only two pitchers during a speech. La Follette's only weakness lay in the fact that once he got wound up in his message he always continued an hour longer than seemed necessary to make his point. One weary farmer in the Midwest, bug-eyed at La Follette's gigantic thirst, commented pointedly: "Holy smokes, this is the first time I ever seen a gas engine run on water!"

An outstanding lecturer of the circuits was Russell H. Conwell, whose inspirational discourse *Acres of Diamonds* was delivered 6000

Above: *William Jennings Bryant, greatest "Mother, Home and Heavener" of them all is fourth from left in this Chautauqua group portrait. Note palm leaf fan.* **Below:** *Edgar Bergen and Charlie McCarthy (left) were among the illustrious names that began the climb to fame on the Redpath circuit.*

125

times, on Chautauqua platforms and elsewhere. Dr. Conwell, sweeping aside all romantic folderol, exhorted his listeners to "get rich—for you have no right to be poor." Love was a fine thing, he asserted, but the lover who had plenty of shekels was a dozen lengths ahead of the pack. And there was no need to go wandering to find the greenbacks; the man worthwhile could find them right in his own back yard.

Dr. Conwell's back yard was obviously the lecture platform, where he amassed a fortune, most of which he used in a philanthropic manner. Following each lecture, he mailed a substantial check to some deserving young man whose name appeared on a list which he carried in his wallet. Dr. Conwell's generosity helped many impecunious boys through college. Later in his life, Dr. Conwell founded Temple University in Philadelphia.

Another surefire Chautauqua speaker was Ralph Parlette, whose lecture, "The University of Hard Knocks," was illustrated by a dramatized message, a forerunner of today's television commercial. The product that Parlette plugged was not soap, but Success, and his visual gimmick was a large glass filled with beans and walnuts. This device represented "The Jar of Life," and the beans and walnuts, he declared with a straight face, were people. Parlette would shake the jar with the vigorous technique of a bartender, then point out triumphantly that, no matter how hard he shook, the walnuts always came to the top and stayed there. The walnuts were the truly big fellows of this dog-eat-dog world, but the poor beans were the tiny, spineless characters with no ambition. Parlette's message boiled down to the seemingly incontrovertible fact that if a little guy wanted to get to the top, he would have to change his size and become a walnut.

Thunderous music from gleaming brass horns stirred the blood, and opened the pocketbook of every skinflint in town.

Nine tents were needed for seven programs in seven towns for seven days.

"An Analysis of Success and Failure" was the broadside aimed at his audiences by "Gatling Gun" Fogleman, who fired 300 words a minute and never paused to reload. Possibly no one understood the burden of his lightning message, but his listeners, the children in particular, were delighted by his gymnastics. Only Billy Sunday surpassed Fogleman in platform acrobatics.

On the list of "select folks" among Chautauqua speakers, we find Carveth Wells, the explorer; Drew Pearson, columnist and commentator; Jane Addams, of Hull House; Judge Ben F. Lindsey (*before* his association with "companionate marriage"); Vilhjalmur Stefansson, the explorer; Richard Halliburton, author and swimmer of the Hellespont; and Captain Richmond Pearson Hobson, hero of Santiago. And from the White House to the platform came Taft, Harding, Coolidge and Hoover. The list of celebrities available is almost without end.

In 1920, the illustrious Winston Churchill, never dreaming of even greater eminence to come, crossed the Atlantic with a contract to address Chautauqua audiences. Doubtless this courageous fighter would have been a tremendous drawing card, had it not been for an unscheduled bout with a New York taxicab, which Mr. Churchill lost. Obliged to spend his allotted American weeks as a patient instead of a trouper, the beloved Britisher never did appear on the circuit.

The inspirational speakers lured many dollars into the till, but before any Chautauqua chain could send them on the road, there was important business to be done. The most active and widespread organization was the Redpath de Luxe Circuit, which exacted a $2100 guarantee from each town along the route. The responsibility of raising that amount, through

Ralph Parlette plugged Success with a large jar filled with beans and walnuts.

the sale of season tickets, rested upon the leading businessmen of the community. If the specified amount was not collected by showtime, the city fathers who signed the contract were pledged to make up the deficit from their own wallets. Redpath and other managements graciously pocketed all the cash resulting from the sale of single admission tickets; important sugar, even by today's standards.

While the management guaranteed the talent, tent, advertising and programs, the town promised police protection and a satisfactory location for the Chautauqua tent. In most localities, finding a large, level piece of ground was no problem, but from time to time the tent crews found themselves faced with complications. The late Moroni Olsen, an actor who headed a dramatic company, described a difficulty of that kind.

"In one town in the Midwest," said Mr. Olsen, "there was only one possible place for the big tent to be erected—an ancient, abandoned graveyard on the outskirts of the community. The area was studded with headstones, and naturally it would have been indelicate to remove them. The tent boys scouted around until they located the spot containing the least number of stones—five or six I think—and erected the tent with the stones sticking up inside like sore thumbs. The trouble was," chuckled Olsen, "when we made our entrances on the stage, we found ourselves facing a crumbling gravestone marked with the disconcerting legend: 'Rest In Peace.' I must say it was rather difficult to play comedy under those grisly circumstances."

Despite such occasional perplexities, a job as a member of a tent crew was the goal of many a young man. While Chautauqua was at its height, ambitious college boys all over the land knew exactly the kind of work they wanted to do during summer vacations. Several million undergraduates shared the same ambition, and each year spent a good part of the spring semester angling for the 6000 openings that would become available when the hot months arrived.

The employment provided by the Chautauqua circuits was alluring, for it was considered an adventure to travel from town to town as one of the custodians of the big tent.

On the economic side, a job with a touring company was ideal for a student, for he could earn as much as $20 a week while seeing the country. There was romance in the work too, for the tent boys were admired by the local belles, and frequently envied by all the citizens of each community in which the Chautauqua tented down for a seven-day stay.

Chautauqua offered employment to young women as well as young men, not only as entertainers but also as managers, contract bookers and general, all-around diplomats. It was discovered by the managers that a pretty girl could often be more persuasive than a fast-talking male when it came to selling the contract to the leading citizens of towns along the circuits.

One of the smartest moves ever made by the managers was the creation of the "Story-Hour Girl," or as she was sometimes designated, "The Junior Chautauqua Girl." This young lady was the forerunner of today's invaluable family adjunct, the baby-sitter. The Junior Chautauqua Girl, like the boys of the tent crew, arrived in town on the opening day and stayed through the week. Usually a college student or school teacher, her function was to gather the local small fry under her wing so that their parents could soak up culture, unencumbered by wriggling youngsters. Early on the first morning, the bright-faced young lady would announce that she was taking over the little ones and would spend the week instructing them in birdwatching, woodlore and the language of the flowers. In her spare time she would rehearse them for their participation in the dramatic Indian Pageant on the final day. Sure enough, when the last day came, the proud parents would assemble to admire their wee Willies and tiny Marys, as they ugh-ed and how-ed around the wigwams and council fires. Some seasons, for a change of pace, the pageant would be Hawaiian in flavor,

Chautauqua orator Ralph Parlette.

the Indian feathers and tomahawks then being supplanted by grass skirts and ukuleles. The Junior Chautauqua Girl did her job up brown, and everyone was pleased save the harassed young lady herself, who doubtless took an oath at the end of the season never to marry and raise hellions of her own.

While the youngsters enjoyed Chautauqua for its war bonnets and hulas, their parents relished it chiefly for its music. Brass bands, always received with enthusiasm, were responsible for hundreds of extra admissions at the ticket entrance. The excitement began early on opening day, when the train pulled into the depot and dark-skinned men in splendid uniforms assembled on the platform, raised their instruments and marched up Main Street to the Commercial Hotel. The thunderous music that emerged from the gleaming horns stirred the blood, sent delicious shivers up the spine, and opened the pocketbooks of all the skinflints in town.

Every afternoon and evening program began with a half-hour musical prelude, both vocal and instrumental. "The Road To Mandalay" reverberated through many a tent, while "The Pilgrims' Chorus," "Poet and Peasant," and "The Stars and Stripes Forever" often competed with the booming of summer thunderstorms. Performances of "The Mikado" and "Robin Hood" with real scenery brought magic to the patrons. "Oh, Promise Me," "The Rosary," "My Hero," and "Ave Maria," performed by professionals, sent them home with stars in their eyes.

Chautauqua music was made by all conceivable kinds and combinations of instruments and artists—from bands to banjos—from vocal trios, quartets and sextets to world-famous opera singers, "fresh from triumphal appearances in the operatic centers of the world." Madame Schumann-Heink, the prima donna of the Metropolitan Opera, traveled so extensively on the circuits that she was known familiarly but lovingly as Madame Human Shanks.

Swiss yodelers, "imported directly from the snow-clad Alpine regions," tickled the customers with their novel vocal gymnastics, and many a small boy drove his parents to distraction by his attempts to master the "o-lee-o-lay-hee" technique in the family parlor. Foreign groups in native costumes, playing unfamiliar instruments, held audiences spellbound, while Negro singers from the Deep South soothed them with religious folk songs, known to them ever afterward as spirituals.

Male quartets were always welcome on Chautauqua bills, the most popular in some parts of the country being the Dunbars, the Weatherwax Brothers and the Whitney Brothers. The Whitneys—Alvin, William, Yale and Edwin—born a generation too soon for television, would surely have profited today in that medium, for they were received as celebrities wherever they appeared. Ed Whitney, who later became a radio producer, once spoke wistfully about the good old days when he and his brothers were brown-tent favorites. "Each of us gained at least ten pounds every summer.

Chautauqua was run as a gigantic assembly

Not because we ate so well in the local beaneries, Lord knows, but because the housewives showed their appreciation of our work by bringing us homemade pies and cakes. Toward the end of the summer we always had to hunt up the town tailor and have our trousers let out at the waist. Then we'd starve our bellies back into shape all winter, so we wouldn't look like an elephant quartet the following season."

The recipe for the ideal Chautauqua program called for one part lectures and two parts music, variety and dramatics. The dramatics opened an exciting new world to rural Americans, for they had been raised in the belief that anything pertaining to the theatre was downright wicked, and therefore to be eschewed. Early in the game even Shakespeare was shunned in performance, although a plain reading of a Shakespeare play was permitted. Years went by before actual performances were given by troupes of actors. Meanwhile dramatic works were literally read, by one person who carried a copy onto the platform, sat down and began with Act I, Scene I.

Shakespeare, as presented by the Ben Greet Players from England, was finally considered morally sound, and soon other companies were offering more current "character-building" plays such as "Cappy Ricks," "It Pays To Advertise," and "Turn To The Right." The latter piece, by reason of its stalwart moral teachings, became the warhorse of the circuits.

In order for a Chautauqua to hold its audience for a full week, it was necessary for the management to offer a diversified program, and to let the customers know before the big show hit town what treasures were in store for them. For weeks preceding the happy day, signs on fences, trees and telephone poles, and banners strung across Main Street proclaimed the fact that big doings were just around the corner. The three golden words "Chautauqua Is Coming" prompted many a farm and small town family to rearrange its time and budget, for Chautauqua was an event not to be missed. For weeks it was anticipated; then for seven days it was enjoyed; and finally it was discussed—long after the big brown tent had been struck and the last of "the talent" had waved farewell from

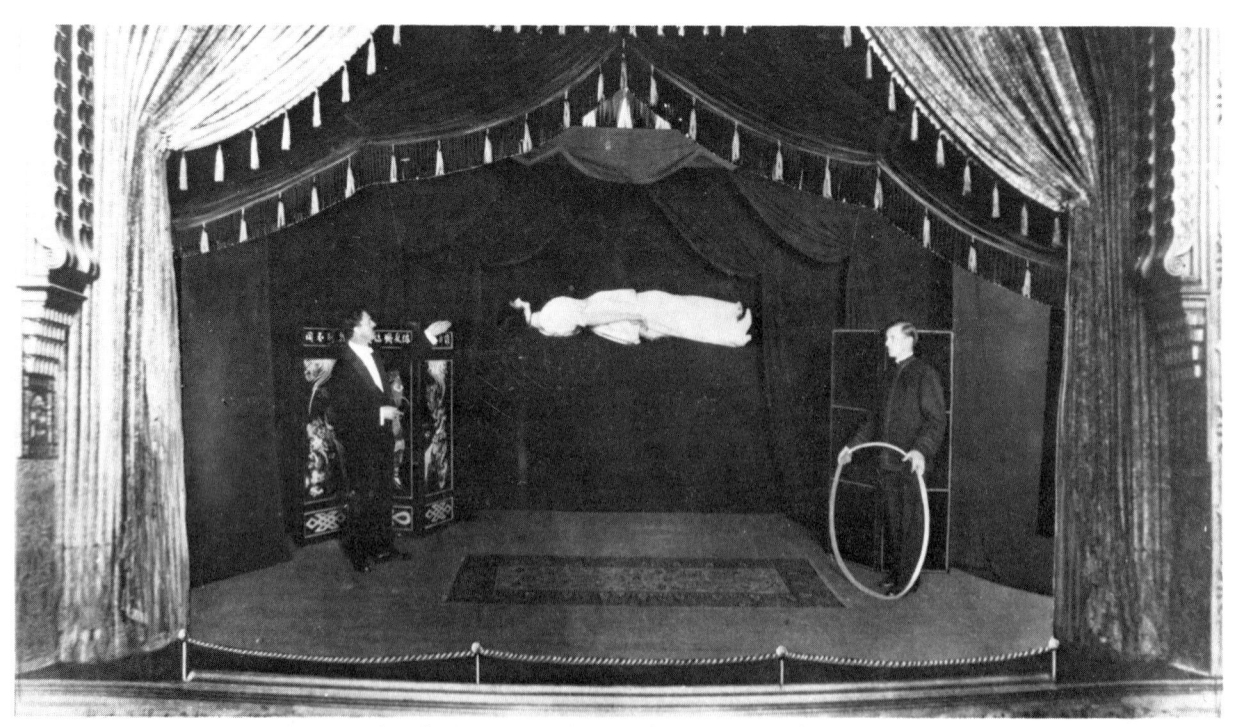

An amazing levitation performed by "Laurant the Magician."

line — on a man-killing schedule.

"The Talent" included this dapper and energetic group of Swiss Bell Ringers.

the rear platform of the moving train.

For the talent, too, there was excitement at the prospect of a summer on the road. Before taking the plunge, the troupers of one unit would assemble for a farewell party, usually in a large city hotel. There were new comedy routines to display; new costumes, songs, and magic tricks. At the end of the merry-making, the First Day Talent boarded the rattler for the next day's opening performance in town number one, out there somewhere in the great dark void. Later the Second Day Talent took to the road; then the Third, Fourth, Fifth, Sixth, and Seventh. After the performance in town one, the First Day Talent caught the night train to become the First Day Talent of town two, and it would remain First Day Talent right down the line, throughout the steaming summer. The talent of the six other days followed suit, and once the season got under way the artists of the different days seldom saw each other again until the season was over. All were encased in the straitjacket of a man-killing schedule.

The gigantic assembly line was now in operation—it had required an army of canny planners to get it whipped into working order. Nine tents were needed to house seven programs in seven different towns for seven days. The tents, as well as the talent, leap-frogged each other constantly, and it was miraculous that the plan worked successfully. Minor complications arose, of course, but they were usually of a personal nature.

Emory Parnell, who, with his family, toured the circuits in a musical act, recalled many a small crisis that loomed large at the time. "One of our toughest problems," said Parnell, "was getting our laundry done. If a bundle got left behind, it never caught up with us again, unless we played the same town the next year. But the local establishments were pretty good about saving our bundles for us. In most cases they'd tuck them away on a top shelf and reach them down for us when we came back 12 months later. Of course, if we didn't come back the next season, the laundry owners were ahead of the game by a couple of shirts and a few dainty underthings."

For the most part, however, the talent was well-behaved and gave audiences their money's worth of pure entertainment of a kind that never before had been served to rural Americans. While city folks attended theatres to catch their vaudeville acts, the people of the hinterland had variety delivered to their doorsteps. And it was variety from A to Z—accordionists to zither-players.

On the first day, musicians and mind-readers held the stage, whetting the patrons' appetites for the performers who were to follow. Twice each day for a full week, eager crowds assembled to be entertained by banjoists, whistlers, bell ringers, jugglers, bird-trainers, yodelers, magicians and musical-saw virtuosos.

Research uncovers a number of familiar names on Chautauqua talent lists. Edgar Bergen, for example, assisted even then by Charlie McCarthy, convulsed many an audience gathered under the big tent. A student at Northwestern University, Bergen began his climb to stardom on the Redpath Circuit in 1922. His first assignment was to entertain the children while their parents were absorbing culture elsewhere. When the news got around that the ventriloquist was more amusing than some of the main attractions, the adults who had come to Bergen's tent to deliver their children refused to leave. Mr. Bergen's reputation and salary climbed quickly, and before long he was performing on the large platform with the élite. The rest, as the fellow said, is history.

A Chicago Redpath program of 1916 contains the name of Louella O. Parsons, a lady who continued westward to discover an even richer Eldorado. The nature of Miss Parson's work in Chautauqua is not revealed in the program, but we may assume that she was neither a juggler nor a Swiss bell ringer.

The researcher in Chautauqua talent may find his curiosity aroused upon discovering the name of an actor who was ingenuously billed as "the handsomest man in the world." One wonders how the late Conrad Nagel felt subsequently about that early description of his well-known countenance.

The name Chic Sale on the Chautauqua roster is an eyebrow-raiser, for Mr. Sale's subsequent best-selling monograph on back-yard architecture seems slightly at odds with the moral, uplifting spirit of the Movement. Further study, however, brings the comforting knowledge that in those early days Chic Sale was a specialist only in "character studies."

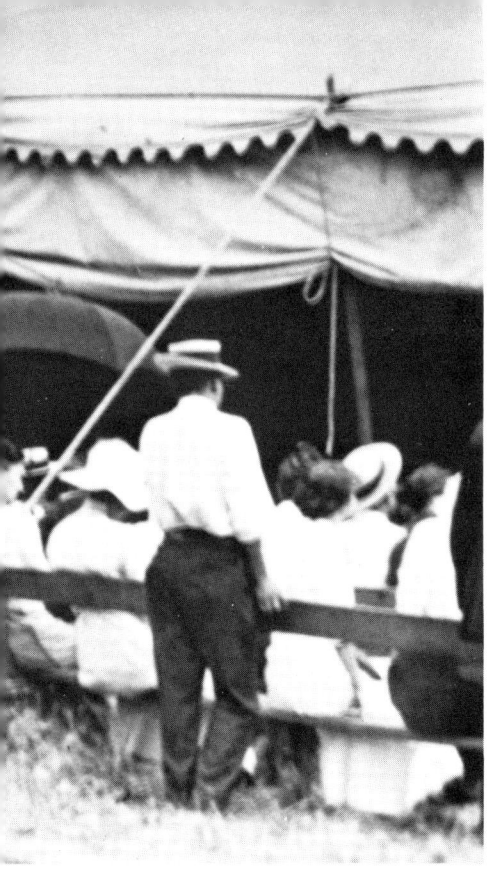

"...get rich — for you have no right to be poor."

Chautauqua exchanged culture for cash in 12,000 communities each summer, entertaining approximately 30 million people yearly.

Author-humorist Irvin S. Cobb was a big man in Chautauqua, big not in drawing power alone, but in physical proportions as well. His audiences always expected, and received, his time-honored opening remark as he lumbered out upon the sagging platform and planted his barrel-like body beside the rostrum. "I come before you in a business suit," grinned Cobb, "but I want you to know that I've been, shall we say—coopered—for a tuxedo."

After the oratory, entertainment, and beautiful music had died away, Chautauqua Week was over, all too soon. On closing night the tent was crowded with people, weary but still game, every one of them stimulated by seven days of marvelous sights and sounds. At some moment during the program, usually following a stirring band number, the manager of the unit appeared on the platform to announce the names of leading citizens who had guaranteed financially that Chautauqua would return the following summer. Each name brought a riffle of applause. Finally, when the manager asked how many in the audience would purchase season tickets next year, every person in the tent raised his handkerchief and waved it in "The Chautauqua Salute."

In the morning only memories remained of the week of glory. Business and household chores were done quietly throughout the long day. During the evening, after supper, the grown-ups wandered slowly down to the empty lot where the big brown tent had stood, and shared a deep sense of loneliness. A few Chautauqua pennants still fluttered on Main Street, but they too looked lonely and forlorn.

Only the children, it seemed, took the loss in their stride, refusing to wear their parents' mantle of gloom. For they had work to do—work that would keep them busy for the remainder of the summer. In barns and back yards, but more often in the dusty field where the tent had been, small boys juggled pop bottles or tried handstands until their arms ached, while their sisters practiced Hawaiian dances or declaimed (just like the beautiful acting lady in the flowing white robe):

> The quality of mercy is not strain'd,
> It droppeth as the gentle rain from
>   heaven . . .

Ralph Parlette, if he had returned for a day, would have been proud of those young ones, for each tiny bean in town seemed to have acquired, by some magic, the makings of a mighty walnut.

END

Slowest of the Slow

Farmer Wilmont's "Slowpoke."

Twenty-five dollars to the slowest horse to trot the half-mile track...

by William H. Sanders

COUNTY FAIR

Years ago, when there were no automobiles, the horse and wagon was man's chief means of getting about. Attention was given to the type of horse that could do this quickly. There was a good market for horses, and almost every farmer was raising colts. There was always a chance for a "fast one." Certain crosses did bring this about, and it was big money for someone.

One year the Brattleboro (Vermont) Fair came up with an offer for a little excitement. Twenty-five dollars to the horse that could take up the most time going around the half mile track and still keep trotting. The directions were to use any two-wheeled vehicle and enter the horses the day of the slow race. When the exciting moment came, twenty horses lined up for the word "go." Some were plump and slick. Others skinny and rough. They had come in from Vermont, New Hampshire, and a few up from Massachusetts.

Farmer Wilmont had driven over from Ludlow, Vermont and entered a rough old sway-back horse under the name of "Slowpoke." He was hitched to a two-wheeled, heavy road cart, one that would carry two people. Considerable fun was made of the get-up by the crowd along the side rails at the starting point. Wilmont was mouthy but took it all in stride. He said "Oh, he is a good hoss. He belongs to the Sooner breed—sooner stand than go."

It was understood that when a horse once slowed to a walking pace, he was automatically out of the race. When the bell sounded, all started off in a flurry. Then the thing was to slow the horses down to an even pace. Wilmont was noisy, kept shouting, "Get a-going Slowpoke, you'll never make it around." Then there would be a few cracks from the lash whip. This excited most of the other horses, which was not a help. Slowpoke made his feet go fast enough, but they had a way of coming down almost in the same place they came up. His advance was very little. Wilmont would shout, "Cheer-up old boy, you might make it." Then there would be a crack of the lash whip under Slowpoke's belly. The old horse would just switch his tail and keep dog-trotting along. Then Wilmont shouted again: "Pick them up and put them down if you ever expect to get there."

When they rounded the half-way post, about half of the drivers had given up the chase. Their horses had defaulted or "began acting up." As the last horse pulled away from Slowpoke, Wilmont cried, "Tell the judge I hope to get there some day." Slowpoke did make it—still trotting. This was no photo finish. There was a good 200-foot margin.

The horse race judge and the Fair officials declared Wilmont and his Slowpoke the winner. There was much fun and joking among racing fans. Considerable bet money changed hands. It was declared a lively afternoon at the annual weekend Brattleboro Fair. That night as Farmer Wilmont and his friend who had come along rode back over the hills to Ludlow, Wilmont observed, "$25.00 isn't bad for a day of excitement and fun." The year was 1910.   END

The author's ice crew and their horses pose on the frozen Kennebec River. Twenty to thirty pair of horses were used.

Courtesy Vicki Woodward Patterson

A Day on the Kennebec

by L.B. Woodward

At five a.m., it was just twenty below — no wind, but still it took strong willpower to get out of that warm bed...

ICE CUTTING

In the early 1900s, Maine farmhouses were generally heated by wood-burning stoves. With few exceptions, bedrooms were unheated, though they were sometimes so arranged that they got some warm air from adjoining rooms, or, if upstairs, from small registers cut through the floor to the heated rooms below. My younger brother, Dorr, and myself had a room over what served as a kitchen-dining room during the cold winter months. When there was a good fire in the kitchen stove, we got a little warm air through the floor register.

January nights were long, cold and dark, except when the moon intervened with its cold, clear light. The creaking sounds caused by the work of frost on timbers, boards, and the nails which held them together were all that broke the quiet.

On such a night I suddenly found myself awake, and wondering what had awakened me. It must be the middle of the night, I thought, and snuggled down into the deep featherbed for more sleep. Then a rooster crowed, and another, and another. Now roosters do crow in the early morning, but it couldn't be morning! These roosters were certainly crowing out of order, and again I settled into the featherbed. I was just drowsing off when I heard my father come into the room below, open the drafts of the stove, and put in more wood. I heard him go out through the shed and open the rolling door (a door hung on hangers with trucks that rolled on a track). I knew then he had gone to the barn to feed horses and cattle.

He usually arose at five o'clock at this time of the year, and I knew it was morning after all. Not long after, I heard my mother come into the kitchen to prepare breakfast. Soon the odor of fried ham and boiling coffee came up through the register. Next, there was the tapping of a broomstick against the register, to which I responded, "Yes, I'm awake."

It took strong willpower to get out of that warm bed and into cold clothes, but after several false starts I made it. Without all the buttons in their proper holes, and carrying some outer garments, I rushed downstairs to the warm kitchen. Upon the stove were two large frying pans. One contained large, juicy slices of smoked ham, and the other contained fried potatoes. I proceeded to get properly buttoned, and my boots laced up.

Father came in with a brimming pail of milk and remarked casually, "Just twenty below this morning, but there is no wind."

Mother removed a pan of hot biscuits from the oven, put a plate of doughnuts on the table alongside the ham and potatoes, and we sat down to breakfast. It was nearly six when we finished. Father and I would eat nothing more until noon. He went out to harness the horse while I dressed for my outdoor job on a cold day, as follows: heavy wool socks; boots and overshoes; two wool sweaters over a wool shirt; an interlined double-breasted overcoat that was knee length; thick wool cap with ear laps down; knitted wool scarf wrapped around face and neck; a pair of wool mittens; and over these a pair of leather mittens.

The jingle of bells told me that Father was outside ready to start on the five-mile drive to the ice houses at Cedar Grove on the Kennebec River. With dinner pails in hand, I ventured into the cold morning. Father wore a long sheepskin-lined coat, with a wide fur collar. With his cap well down over his forehead, and the fur collar turned up and closely buttoned, only his eyes, nose and mouth were visible. In the back of the old green pung was a large burlap bag of hay for Kit's lunch. Wrapping a heavy horseblanket around our legs, and tucking in over that a fur robe, we were off. It was still a starlit night, with no sound but the tinkle of the

Cedar Grove, Maine. The men used long-handled picks to manipulate the blocks cut from the river on to the apron of the elevator that carried the ice up into the ice house.

Courtesy Vicki Woodward Patterson

139

On a hot summer's day, children everywhere followed the iceman in hopes of being handed a cool, dripping hunk of ice to suck.

Courtesy Vicki Woodward Patterson

bells, and the creaking of the runners on the hard-packed snow. As we proceeded, other teams joined us, and when we reached the locality of the ice house there was much activity.

There was a long stable, with stalls for perhaps 60 horses. We, and the other "commuters," unharnessed the horses and put them in the stable for the day, while the men who lived at the boarding houses on the river were taking out their horses and getting them paired up for the day's work. At seven o'clock the whistle sounded and men moved out onto the river, or to their places in the huge ice houses where the ice was stored. There were 20 or 30 pairs of horses at work with the men, helping to remove layers of snow on top of the ice with scrapers; and pulling the cutters and groovers which marked the ice off into a sort of checkerboard pattern. The grooves were cut to a depth of eight or ten inches, and rows of blocks were then broken off with "busting bars" and towed to the apron (which was the lower end of the long incline) with its endless chain that carried the ice high enough so that it would slide on "runs" by force of gravity to its ultimate resting place in one of the huge rooms of the ice houses.

My job was holding a scraper. Scraping served two purposes. It removed the accumulated snow from the surface of the ice, so that the ice would freeze to a greater depth (15- to 18-inch thickness was considered desirable) and made possible the marking and grooving of the ice so that blocks of it could be broken off.

A scraper was a dustpan-shaped object, about eight feet wide, made of wood, but having a steel cutting edge, and very shallow steel runners. Extending from the rear were two handles, about three feet apart, which the holder of the

After dinner — out on Old Man River again.

scraper used to control its movements, by lifting, depressing and steering the tool as it picked up, and later dumped, its load of snow. The scraper was pulled by a pair of horses, usually driven by their owner.

Driving out on the river to where the snow had not been removed, the team was headed toward the shore; and as the horses started, the scraper handles were lifted and the snow was pushed into the "dustpan." The depth of the "bite" depended upon the depth of the snow and the judgment of the holder. The scraper loaded, it was pulled over the ice to the shore and dumped. We then drove back for another load. The effort involved depended on the density of the snow. Sometimes when snow and rain together formed "snow ice," it was necessary to plane off the surface to a depth of several inches. The chips thus formed had to be scraped away to the "dumps." This was much harder work. The planer chips were chunks of ice, up to six inches in length, of all shapes, hard to walk in, hard to get the scraper edge to bite into, and were a heavy lift to start the dumping process. It was also bad walking in the dumps when there was a foot or more of planer chips. It was here that at times the horses would get bad hock injuries from the sharp calks on their shoes.

The temperature rose with the sun, but remained in the 'teens all day. This was good weather for putting up ice, as the colder it was when packed in the houses, the better quality when it was taken out the following summer. How many days of scraping were necessary depended on the amount of snow, the number of teams at work, and the size of the field to furnish enough ice.

Sometimes the forenoons seemed long. The best way to judge the time was to know the time schedules of the Maine Central trains which went up and down on the west bank of the river. It was too complicated a procedure to burrow through layers of clothing to look at a pocket watch. Finally the twelve o'clock whistle sounded, and men and horses moved rapidly to the shore. The horses were fed and watered, the men living in the boarding houses went to their places, and the commuters, like Father and me, went to a crude lunchroom where a fire had been kept during the forenoon, to warm the place and the dinner pails.

The lunchroom was long and narrow, with wooden seats along the walls. There was a large box stove near one end, and the stovepipe ran the length of the center of the room, to the far end, at a height of about three feet. Attached to the top of the stovepipe was a shelf about 18 inches wide, which was for two rows of dinner pails. During the forenoon, the keeper of the lunchroom had collected the dinner pails from the vehicles of the commuters, and put them on this shelf to warm the contents. One must know his own dinner pail!

The dinner pail of those days *was* a pail, not a lunch kit. The coffee (or tea) was in the bottom of the pail. Above it was a tray six or seven inches deep, in which was the main course, real he-man sandwiches or their equivalent. Above that was a shallow tray for a large piece of pie, or other dessert. Then the cover, and inverted on a ring soldered to the cover was a tin dipper. Such a pail with attachments was at least a foot tall and had a long bail. The coffee was well heated if the keeper had done his duty. Dinner first, then smokes for the smokers, a few comments on the weather, some tall yarns, and the one o'clock whistle. Out on Old Man River again.

In the afternoon a breeze came up from the northwest, so that the outgoing trip was distinctly unpleasant. The wind was behind us on the return to the dumps. A four o'clock express down gave renewed hope, and at the sound of the five o'clock whistle, even the horses knew that the day's work was ended. There was a general rush to the stables, Kit was hitched to the old green pung, and Father and I were home before six. After a hot supper in a warm room, I went upstairs with my kerosene lamp. Very shortly I was once more well ensconced in that soft bed, with three comforters over me. With the satisfying thought that by my day's work I had added another dollar and a half to my week's pay envelope, I went to sleep.

END

Getting There Was Half the Fun

by Stephen Alexander

When people reminisce about the "Old Snow Train," they're talking about the one *they* traveled on to the New England ski country. Actually, there were many "snow trains", and they fanned out from Boston to Maine, New Hampshire and Vermont. The Boston and Maine operated its first trains as early as 1931, and by 1936 snow trains, running in five or six sections, carried a total of 24,140 passengers. It was, in fact, SUCCESS all the way to World War II, when the snow trains were suspended "for the duration." After the war, for a while it looked as though snow trains would pick up where they had left off and become part of America's postwar boom. But, save for the year 1947, when there were over 20,000 riders to the

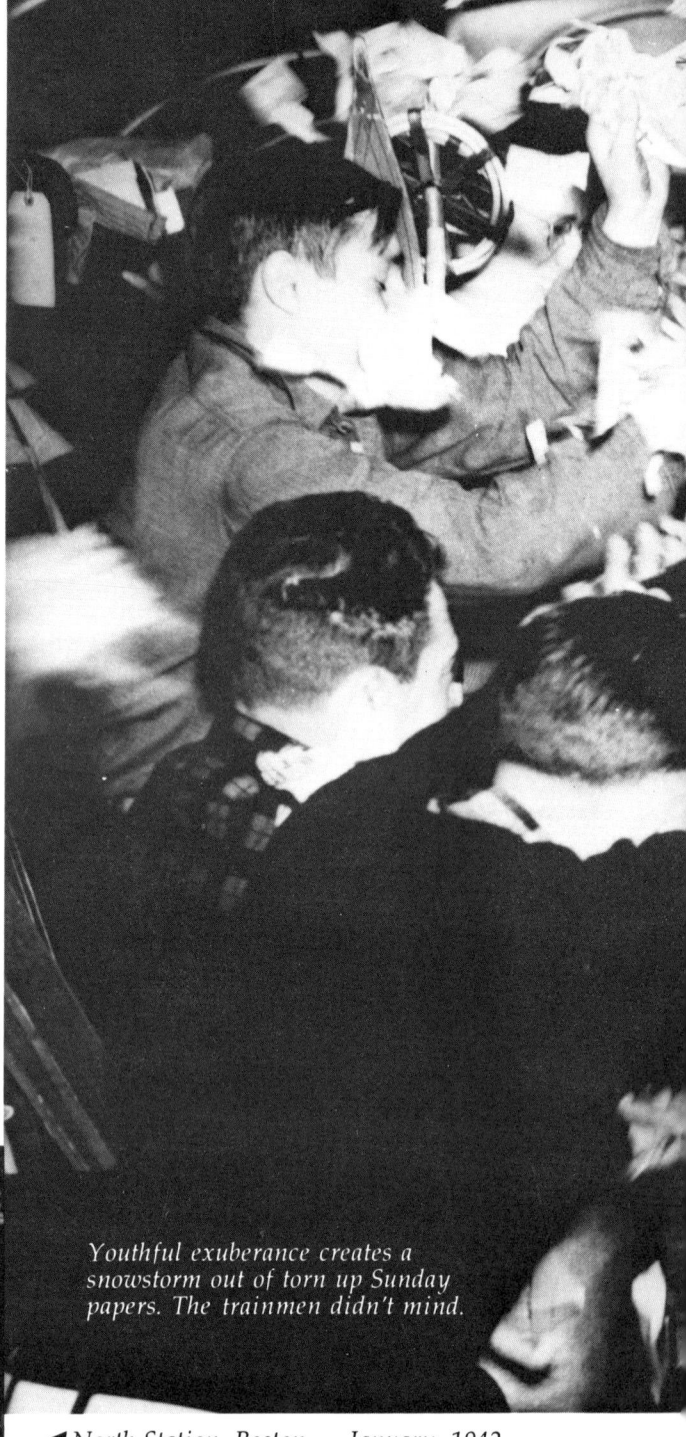

All photos in this chapter by Stanley A. Bauman

Youthful exuberance creates a snowstorm out of torn up Sunday papers. The trainmen didn't mind.

◀ *North Station, Boston — January, 1942.*

SNOW TRAINS

▼ *Rounding a snowy curve, you could see the other end of the train.* ▼ *Dining car, 1936, enroute to the North Country.*

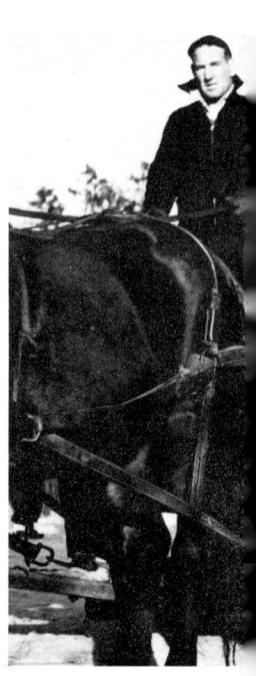

Leaving the train at North Conway (N.H.) in 1942, skiers collect their baggage from the car.

Intervale, New Hampshire, 1930s.

slopes, the snow train's patrons declined slowly to the '50s and rapidly after that. Its arch enemies, the paved highway and the modern automobile, absorbed the majority of its business—buses did their bit, too. Wheels simply reached more places than rails. The skier could leave his home on Friday, enjoy two days on the slopes, and be home by Monday noon. And, apart from convenience, the highway was faster, and that's what really mattered—or so it seemed until 1972, when AMTRAK undertook to restore a snow train to the tracks running through the Connecticut River Valley from New York to Montreal, spurred by the gasoline shortage. Who knows—perhaps the gay and friendly days of the Old Snow Train are slated to return to New England . . . after a snooze of 20 years. END

Skiers on Mount Cranmore, early 1950s.

Horse-drawn pungs conveyed skiers from North Conway station to Mount Cranmore.

Old-fashioned song fest aboard the snow train.

The Glorious Fourth

by Irwin Ross and Melvin Haugan

... as the sun touched the horizon, you lit a No. 2 cannon cracker ...

In 1899, in our old town, no boy ever called Independence Day anything but The Fourth. Next to Christmas, it was our big day of the year.

Once it had been Independence Day, with speeches from a platform, and bells rung, and the Declaration of Independence read. But by 1899, all that was past and The Fourth was ours alone.

The Fourth really began a week or so before, when the stores put on sale firecrackers, caps, torpedoes, toy cannon, and the giant crackers that got bigger and bigger until the law stopped them. I do not remember having saved money for Christmas; but I always saved for The Fourth, because parents could not be counted upon for more than a quarter or so, at most a dollar bill.

They knew that our hoard of pennies, two-cent pieces, nickels, and dimes would never buy more than enough ordinary crackers to keep the day going, plus a few big ones. Whereas one moment of excess generosity on their part would be sure to result in some terrific explosion, with the cat on top of it, or the sides of a box falling all over the neighborhood.

Our ritual for The Fourth was exact. First, up before sunrise, taking care not to wake mother, who might send you back to bed, or sister, who might try to follow you. Under the bed was the shoe box filled with everything you had saved to buy. Grab it carefully and tiptoe through the silent house, stepping over the places where the floor creaked, unbolting the front door softly, then out into a dim and unfamiliar world.

Off the porch, and down the dewy walk, fumbling as you went at the string around the box. Finally you pulled out a pack of crackers; but darn, the plaited fuses just wouldn't unweave!

The first cracker came off fuseless; the second was all right, but you dropped the match. The next match lit her, she sputtered, you threw her high between the maples, when, gosh darn it, a bang came from across the street. Bill Jones had beaten you to it!

But there was another first. It was terribly extravagant, yet something you could talk about all day. Under the syringa bush was a big empty can, hidden there yesterday. Put that in the middle of the street, light a *whole pack* of firecrackers at once, and drop them in. That would wake them. It did.

Boys like little gray ghosts came slipping through the yards or over the fences, listened to the bang-bang for a minute, then went back to their own business. So did you. Now it was pop-pop everywhere.

The family cat peered down from the grape arbor, then sprang out with a flash and bang behind her. A small cannon cracker (you had only six) justified the nickel it cost when it burst in the top of the old cedar, sending a whirl of cheeping sparrows over the sheds and fences. And as the sun touched the horizon, below your parents' window you lit a No. 2 cannon cracker (you had only two of them). What a roar! When heads appeared at the window, you stuck out your tongue and shouted, "Get up—it's The Fourth!" and ran.

The gang was at the top of Jefferson Avenue hill. As you panted up to join them, they were arguing: "It's not time yet" . . . "Yes, it

FIRECRACKERS

is"... "Somebody will brush them off"... "They'll come out and stop us."

Bill Jones, the biggest boy, booted the others into line. Then he took a box of paper percussion caps from each of the kids, redivided them, and sent out working parties. Already we could hear the first horsecar jangling up the hill. Hastily we lined the tracks with caps, then hid behind bushes and fences to wait for the fun.

Soon we heard the driver say "Giddap!" to the horses, heard his black-snake whip snap, heard the car begin to rumble down grade. Then crack, spark, sputter, bang! as the wheels hit a pile of caps.

Up the horses reared, backing, pulling sideways, but the car carried them along and the rails held it. Then off they went at a gallop—streetcar horses at a gallop—tearing down the hill, the car swaying, a woman inside screaming, the driver leaning backward to swear at us as we staggered into the street, doubled up with laughter. It was magnificent.

Then someone yelled, "Cheese it!" There came the Judge out of his doorway, in his nightgown! We scattered like rabbits, beat it over fences, stuck our fists in our mouths. Oh, we'd tell about this for the rest of the year!...

Now we could settle down to ordinary fun. Everyone lit a punk stick and followed his own inclinations. Bury a firecracker and see the dirt fly. Pinch the end of a cracker and fire it in your fingers. Break two and make sissies of them, each opposite each. They would fight like a pair of cats. Boy, this was *really* fun!

Soon it was midmorning, and much quieter. Some of the boys had shot off everything they had, except a few crackers to use as rockets at night. Then some adventurous lad dragged out a big dry goods box, set it on our pavement, and put a cannon cracker No. 1—a No. 1!—under it. I got there just in time to see the box rip and tear up into the sky.

Before the day was over, there was one more item in every boy's ritual for The Fourth. You dragged upstairs to bed, undressed, and opened the window. You could see tiny star bursts over the tree tops from distant rockets, and it was damp outside with a wonderful burnt gunpowder smell.

Then you took a firecracker, the very last one, and lit it in the room, which was forbidden of course, and held it sputtering at the window until the very last second. Then you tossed it out into the dark. The flash and bang made the birds cheep again.

Christmas was only six months away—but it would be a whole year to the next Fourth of July.

END

Iron Character and Where It Came from

by Claire W. Reed

My introduction to iron-willed relatives, iron sink, iron stove and at least nine uncomfortable wooden chairs in that great varnished kitchen was far from my dream of a rose-covered Cape Cod cottage.

Lots of people live on Cape Cod today, and they just love it. Compared to the time I lived there, it has become a part of semi-suburbia in winter, and a melting pot of motels, marinas and money for 10 weeks in the summer.

My Cape Cod introduction was made in the 1940s when, as a young, engaged girl, I was taken from the fast and wicked city to meet my potential in-laws. Never shall I forget my introduction in the great varnished kitchen, where in marital endurance lived Aunt Emma and Uncle Uriah Henry. Two other relatives, Aunt Ethel and Uncle Willie Pickett, also came in to meet their "city-educated" nephew's choice.

After the formalities of "who I was" and "where I come from," I knew they were taking in my thinness, silk stockings, lipstick, regrettable religious affiliation and, more than likely, my lack of warm, sensible underdrawers, which subject was brought up and discussed as: "The girls today don't wear enough to dust a banjo." This witticism came from behind the tobacco-stained whiskers of Uncle Willie Pickett. "Seems a shame. No wonder they all die of the consumption and are thin-blooded." This was from behind the hand of Aunt Ethel to Aunt Emma. I could not protest because I did not own a pair of even knee-length underdrawers, but I was so anxious to please and have them like me, that

Wash day in Cotuit, Massachusetts, at the Adams summer cottage. The child is the photographer's brother, Thomas H. Adams.

Henry Carter Adams photo
Courtesy Dr. William Bake

OLD CAPE COD

Old Cape Cod. From a glass negative labeled "Chatham, Quissett?"

I nodded in complete agreement to everything that was said, suggested or supposed.

This little screening that went on in that enormous kitchen, with its multicolored "art square" on the floor, iron sink, iron stove and iron-willed relatives, and at least nine uncomfortable wooden chairs, was far from my dream of a Cape Cod cottage, complete with roses, hollyhocks, and Joseph C. Lincoln passing the door ready to record its charm.

After that episode, I vowed to "college-educated" husband never to return. The floors were cold, the stoves were cold, the people were cold and, terrible blow, completely indifferent to the charms which I had been brought up to believe I was heavily endowed with.

Life, however, is full of surprises, and my big one was to land about two years later, as a young wife and mother, practically in the middle of that varnished kitchen, with the nine straight chairs, multicolored art squares and other "comforts."

Gone then were the Aunts and Uncles, and baby and I lived in solitary discomfort six days a week, as "college-educated" husband had work which kept him "off Cape" all week. I was filled with the health, heart and high hopes which are usually bestowed upon one at 20 and are usually wasted, but I certainly needed every red corpuscle for the days ahead.

First I found there were the stoves to consider. I had no idea of stoves, how to run them, or how this demanding pair would motivate my every move, since without both of them going strong there was neither heat, hot water nor food. To keep them going strong, one must always rise early and carefully shake down the fire, leaving a nice little bed of hot coals exposed to the draft which you have neatly turned in the stovepipe. Then a little coal is added (gently now, as this stove is temperamental)—a little pea coal, a little nut coal for a tranquilizer. When the blue flame licks up and all the coal gas has gone up the chimney (you hope), you close the draft and all is well!

But if, oh woe, the fire is *out* in the morning, there is a big to-do with paper, kindling, kerosene (if you were daring and distraught), and finally more coal. Every day, too, ashes must be offered up to the altar of the Fire Gods, who, in this case, lived in the ash heap far behind the barn.

A 14-room monstrosity of a house, well calculated to break your back, neck and spirit — all at once...

This 14-room monstrosity in which we struggled to survive the winter was what they'd call today "A House of Ideas." This house had ideas and all terrible ones, calculated to break the back, the neck, and/or the spirit!

Have you ever "greased down" an iron sink about 30 inches high? Have you ever descended the steep, circular stairs of a Cape Cod cellar, where the food was kept in lieu of refrigeration? Have you ever carried baskets of clothes way "up attic," where they were hung to dry in winter? Have you ever dashed out in rain, sleet, wind, hail or hurricane to the dubious comforts of the "outhouse," complete with *Sears Roebuck* catalog of 1923 to peruse at your leisure?

Friends from the city who could go home to tubs of hot, scented bath water, thermostats and indoor plumbing would exclaim: "How quaint, how charming, what you could do with a place like this, what possibilities!" All the while I'd be thinking, "I know what I could do with it all right—*burn it down!*" And one could have, very easily, with all that varnish on walls, floors and art squares! However, pyromania had not set in quite yet for, as in the bottom of Pandora's box, there was that one little parcel marked "hope."

Within the year "hope" turned out to be our own little mortgage-hung cottage, complete with heat, lights, and indoor plumbing which was connected to its own glorious cesspool.

Most of the work on this house was accomplished by the joint efforts of my husband, old Uncle Roger from "up the village" and myself. Uncle Roger, who had the only real knowhow of building, considered us a pair of "educated fools." Of course my husband was one of "them," but he had been "up Boston for a long time and even went clear to New York City once. Not that it never done him much good, far as I can see," to quote Uncle Roger, who put up with our blunderings simply because he couldn't stand to see "a good job, poor done."

But the little house survived our efforts, was built and was charmingly encircled by lilacs in May. These the relatives would come to pick and place on the graves of the departed who slept in proper peace in the sandy, windy little cemetery. The lilacs did not last very long in the preserve jars and milk bottles into which they were jammed, but, as gentle Aunt Manda said, "We want the dead to know they ain't forgot."

It was these lilacs that finally led me to make friends. The relatives and neighbors would consent to "step in" to our new abode and seemed to think it "kinda cozy and fixed up real nice." Often they would come to call, for making "calls" was the only diversion they had outside their homes.

How well I remember the first unheralded visit from the Aunts! There they stood in their second-best dresses, worst of possible hats, cotton stockings of orange hue, sensible shoes and, I assumed, the warm-underwear requisite of good sense and health. These ladies did not possess high style, simple elegance or social elan. I am sure they could have resisted all the efforts of Paris designers because, no matter what new pattern they had or how they tried, all the dresses stitched up on the "Howes," "New Homes" and "Singers" emerged looking somehow the same!

The protocol of the call consisted of first unabashed appraisal of you, your child and your home. Generally they spoke of how thin, or "drawed through a knothole," I looked, how underclad the child was, and what "odd pieces" of furniture we had. Whether or not "odd" was meant to mean the rare and unusual, I do not know, but I sincerely doubt it.

On this first visit, I suggested tea and cookies, but they set me straight for all time. They announced they did not drink tea or any other "stimulants" or eat in the middle of the afternoon. Supper was at five o'clock, dinner had been at noon. "No need" to eat or drink now.

No, they did not eat or drink, but how they loved to sit and talk! These ladies were preoccupied with birth, sickness, trouble and death. A whole afternoon could be given over to the discussion of Mrs. So-and-So up the village who

1898 — the floors were cold, the stoves were cold, and so were the people — 'til you got to know them

Courtesy Arthur Goodenough Collection

was "a great sufferer, the doctor just don't know, her daughter married a no 'count man from New Bedford, which broke her all up, and the child warn't more'n half-witted." Over to Brewster was "Mrs. Abby, whose husband was known to keep a 'fancy woman' and had drove double harness' since they was married!"

Then the births would be discussed. Their own confinements and miscarriages; babies who were born blue, black or with a caul over them, all after long and anguished labors. According to them, there was no such thing as a normal delivery, nor had there ever been one on Cape Cod.

Personalities were analyzed with some attempt at the preservation of charity, but sometimes the peculiar ways of others could not be denied, and they would all agree that "Miss Nettie must be going through the change because she took me off shorter'n pie crust the other day!"

Death by drowning had happened in nearly every family, and it was sad to hear of the loss of so many brothers, husbands and betrotheds. About death they were practical, orderly, neat and ready; and I imagine to die was also something to do in the existence of many who must have inwardly rebelled against monotony!

I remember one little old lady who at 90 lived alone. She scoured her floors with beach sand, she whitewashed her fence, tended her shiny warm stoves and her lovely red geraniums with equal care, and she neatly tagged everything in her house with the name of the person to

Old Cape Cod fisherman, dressed for "weather."

whom it was to go. Her "layin'-out" dress was periodically pressed and sponged, and under the pincushion on her bureau was a sealed note bearing the name of the local undertaker and containing all instructions for the funeral down to the last Amen.

I personally experienced the practical approach to the loss of a loved one and the Cape Codder's stoic way when one morning my phone rang, and it was a neighbor. Now this was a surprise. Cape Codders did not use a phone for "goin' on." It was an instrument purely for emergency, and their telephone manners were so abrupt that if you did not know this to be their way, you'd wonder what you had done to offend. Well, to get back to this practical lady and her call, it went something like this: "This is Mrs. Baker. Will was took real bad early this mornin' and the doctor says it will only be a matter of hours now. I was wonderin' if you'd take his suit up to that quick cleaner in Hyannis. I want to have it ready for the undertaker. It's some spotted."

I said of course I'd go right away; so with baby and potential shroud we went to Hyannis, had the suit "quick cleaned" and hurried back.

I was on time. "Will," she announced, "is gone." Then she took the suit. "How much?" the widow wanted to know. I said to please think nothing of it, I was pleased to help in some small way at such a sad time. But this little lady, whose poor Will lay in the other room, insisted upon paying her debts. She wanted "nothing plaguing her." So I told her the charge for cleaning the suit. Plainly she was aghast, for she had not dealt in the luxuries of the dry cleaner. "Well they got some ginger chargin' prices like that even in the middl'er winter!"

The lady was also, shall we say, emotionally restrained. She had buried two husbands, at 75 she took a third, with whom it was said she "took great comfort," and they passed their winters in Florida.

One winter third husband suddenly died, and I got the news "up the Post Office"—first source of gossip, hearsay and mail. "Hear Gorham died down in Florida," said my informer, who was the local handyman. "Just got penny postcard from Sadie. She's shippin' his ashes up parcel post, I guess. Wants me to bury 'im next the other two husbands, and leave a spot for her in the middle. I hate to think of diggin' that hole, the ground's so durned froze!"

Come summer they all had means of earning a "little extry," for everyone took in boarders or rented rooms, and give credit, the rooms were spotless, "reasonable," and well inspected daily when they "did 'em up!"

Confidences were exchanged concerning the neatness or disorder of their "guests." They talked about the amount of lace and frills on the lady's underwear, the face creams, paint and powder on her bureau and, "I *think she smokes* and he's got a *whiskey bottle* hidden somewheres!"

When the fall came, and the summer folk went back to their cities, the ladies of the church would begin to have their "sews." At these affairs things were made to sell to next summer's crop. They tied quilts, crocheted covers for everything in the world, made holders, "aprons that went round ya," and embroidered pillowcases that would leave you cut and bruised if you ever tried to rest a weary head on the abundance of French knots, lazy-daisy stitches and "tattin'" which adorned them.

At the sews, they'd discuss their experiences with the summer folk, and final consensus was, "they all smoke like chimneys, wore no clothes to amount to nothin', turned day into night and night into day, drove like fools, drank booze, and weren't more'n half-witted!"

Yes, those years on Cape Cod were ones of revelation and introduction to an old order that hath now changeth! Sometimes I miss the little house, the lilacs, the sea winds, whispering scrub pine, the mayflower's indescribable sweetness, and the ways of those plain folk.

Never can we go back to the Uriahs, Gorhams, Netties, Sadies and Wills, for they are in Heaven and I am sure in neatly sponged and pressed dresses and dry-cleaned suits, sitting in composure on their clouds, making certain there are no frivolous angels, no wasteful ones, or angels who fly too high or too fast!

And what must they think of the satellites and astronauts who threaten their new domain! I can hear them now, Miss Nettie to Cousin Ethel, "Why can't they mind their business, stay where the Good Lord put 'em, and do an honest day's work. There's just this much about it, Ethel, the rest, it's all nothin'!"   END

Last of Its Kind
by Ernest H. Cole

Dad escaped drowning by a whisker, I learned a bitter lesson in sportsmanship, and two live skunks carried off the honors.

When I was a boy, my father owned the general store and was postmaster in Prospect Harbor, Maine. From this small coastal village one could look out on the broad Atlantic and watch the sailing ships as they plied their trade up and down the coast.

Population of the village was under 500, and the residents, as a rule, had to provide their own entertainment. Hunting wild game was enjoyed by practically all the males and they usually climaxed the season with a Community Hunting Match.

Our village held one just before Thanksgiving, November, 1900, which, in so far as I know, was the last of its kind—and it was a thriller. Dad escaped drowning by a whisker, I cheated and got a bitter lesson in sportsmanship, and two live skunks carried off the honors.

An organized hunting bee, so popular throughout New England at one time, is now history. It was a one-day affair and won by the team which posted the highest tally—for example: 10,000 points for a deer or bear, 5,000 for a fox, 1,000 for grouse or skunk, 100 for sea bird or rabbit, and so on. Watchers saw that all game was killed the day of the match, proof being a fresh nose, ear, or head.

For days this upcoming event was the talk of the village. Guns were cleaned, hundreds of shells loaded, maps drawn of areas most likely to shelter game, and the women discussed their choicest recipes for the banquet.

"Tomorrow's the big day," chorused the Nimrods, as names were drawn from a hat to form the two competing teams. Only a few winks of sleep were caught before day brightened in the east and the hunters took to woods, fields and sea. All day long the banging of guns sounded like a raging battle.

Long before daybreak, on that cold November morning, my father and two other gunners rowed a dory, using oars, three miles to sea and landed on "black ledge," so called, where sea birds rafted to feed. Two men set the decoys and threw the guide line toward the rocks, but it fell short.

In the darkness, Dad, who was ashore, couldn't see and stepped forward to pick up the reel, and down he went over his head in that ice-cold water. His 225 lbs. plus heavy soaked clothing was too much. He couldn't swim, and they couldn't pull him into the boat; so by hooking his legs over the gunwales and hanging to the stern they towed him around the ledge to a safe landing. The others shared what dry clothing they could spare; then they bagged

HUNTING BEE

Author Ernest H. Cole at Prospect Harbor, Maine — November, 1900.

50 coots (no game limit then)—a 5,000 tally for their team.

Being only just a Nimrod, I tagged along with an older hunter, Rich Bendix. At a place called Roaring Brook, Rich said, "Under that big pine tree across the brook you'll find a porcupine that John Noonan and I shot two days ago. Skin off his nose. I won't say anything." In my enthusiasm it did not occur to me that Noonan was captain of the other side, so I followed the suggestion and turned in a nose for 1,000 points.

As twilight faded, a November chill settled which only sharpened the atmosphere for the hunters who brought their game to the community hall to be counted. As they checked in, tallies were posted. First one side would be ahead, then the other. Excitement ran high.

The hammer was just about to fall, ending the match, when along came Billie Seavey pushing a wheelbarrow on which was a wire trap containing two live skunks. Howls of protest went up. Game must be killed to count.

"All right," said Billie, "I'll kill them now right here in the yard."

But for obvious reasons the objections were even louder! Finally they were admitted and the 2,000 points won the match.

After a bountiful supper, furnished by the Ladies Improvement Society and paid for by the losing side, hunters gathered at the general store to discuss the match. The potbellied stove was stoked to a fiery red, the hanging kerosene lamps cast a mellow glow over the red-shirted group; tall tales of where they went, what they saw and the "one that got away" were almost as exciting as the hunt itself.

When the conversation died down, John Noonan, who sat quietly smoking his pipe, asked an innocent question. "Who went with Rich Bendix to-day?"

Silence, but I felt my face getting red.

Someone spoke up, "Why, Ernest went with Rich."

"Did Ernest turn in a porcupine?"

By that time my guilt was so evident that I stood convicted.

My embarrassment, however, was relieved when Billie Seavey began to laugh and all eyes focused on him.

"About those skunks," said Billie, "I hate to tell you fellers, but I trapped them when they were babies and cut out the scent bags. Now they make nice pets."

END

Rolling the Roads
by Henry N. Andrews, Jr.

One hundred and fifty years ago, snow plowing equipment in New England simply did not exist—

SNOW-ROLLERS

Snow-roller with a six-horse hitch at the top of the hill in Dublin, New Hampshire. About 1920.

It is not often that events dating back little more than three-quarters of a century may arouse much enthusiasm on the part of the antiquarian. The story of the snow-roller seems to be that of an in-between—it is hardly old enough to be history, yet its memory is fast fading from a very sketchily recorded page in the past of New England. Representing as it does a transitional stage between the snowbound winters of a little more than a century ago and the present era of clean-swept highways, its memory seems worthy of perpetuating.

Until quite recently, one could still occasionally find in the sheds where the town's road

Above: *Out in the country you'd often need all the horses and all the weight you could get after a heavy fall.* **Below:** *An ox-drawn roller was a rare sight. This one is in Salisbury, New Hampshire — 1910.*

...it was often necessary to run a harrow over the roads in early spring...

service equipment is stored an old snow-roller, bulky and ponderous in appearance, yet a decidedly picturesque and unique answer to the problem of winter travel of a few decades back. A few may exist today, but most have gone the way of those things of the past which no longer serve a useful purpose. They have been broken up for lumber or simply left to molder back into the forest soil.

From the early 1630s, when settlers of the territory that was to be called New Hampshire began to move in from the coast, the prospects of snowbound weeks and months each winter were not anticipated with any great delight. The larger streams, when thoroughly frozen, often served as useful thoroughfares for horse drawn sleds, but at best they were precarious and the casualty list is a long one. But beyond these frozen aquatic highways, there could be but little travel in the early days when the snow began drifting in for the winter.

It was only when the automobile became the main means of local transportation that the problem of eliminating snow from the roads and highways began to be most pressing. Prior to that time, a reasonable accumulation of snow, so long as it was fairly uniform, made a desirable roadbed for sleighs, pungs, and the like—with rubber tires, of course, things were different.

One hundred and fifty years ago, snow plowing equipment in New England, at least, was nonexistent. Following a heavy snow fall, eight to twenty yoke of cattle were teamed together, without any plowing implement behind them, and simply driven along the roads, the number of animals involved depending on the amount of snow that had fallen and the depth of the drifts. With the larger teams, one man was in charge of every three yoke. A considerable share of the burden of course fell on the leading yoke and for this reason it was necessary to change it frequently. This method of "plowing" undoubtedly left much to be desired but it at least rendered possible travel of a sort over the main thoroughfares.

Later, when sleds were in more general use, the efficiency improved somewhat. A log eight to ten feet long was fastened on to one side of a sled and a block of wood on the other side. The log served for weight and the block of wood as a means of increasing the width of the plowed path. So far as I have been able to ascertain, in this earliest use of a sled as an implement of clearing the roads, the log was used only as additional weight while the front of the sled diverted such snow as it might to one side or the other. The sled, moreover, served to transport the cider barrel—a function that is said to have been esteemed rather highly!

Apparently, the tremendous and easily-manipulated power needed by a plow to move snow effectively from the roads had to await the coming of the gasoline motor. Therefore, instead of removing the snow, the next best step was taken—since it could not be scraped off, why not pack it down? And to accomplish this, rolling equipment of sorts began to take over the job. According to S. A. Weeks of Pittsburg, New Hampshire, the first roller in that region was a large birch log with wooden plugs in the ends, the latter serving to attach a simple frame. It is not surprising that birch should have been selected in view of the smoothness and uniformity of the trunk, and in the virgin forests of old New Hampshire, occasional canoe birches of ponderous girth have been reported. Trees up to six feet in diameter once existed in the state, although such specimens were undoubtedly exceptional.

This relatively simple device was followed by larger oak rollers built on a framework of iron. These came into use in central and northern New Hampshire about 1895. The rollers apparently attained rather sudden and widespread popularity during the late 1800s and early part of this century. A roller six feet in diameter was in use in Pittsburg in 1896 and a smaller one a few years later. The first roller used in Sanbornton, in central New Hampshire, was in 1906 and was built by Walter A. Wilson of Laconia, who has kindly supplied a few facts about their construction and cost.

An early method of "breaking out" a road was to use a heavy "scoot" attached to a sled. Garland Road, Rye, New Hampshire.

Courtesy Eleanor M. Garland

Although some of the rollers were built entirely of wood, others, seemingly of a more durable nature, were built on stout iron wheels at either end of the rollers.

The dimensions of what seems to be a fairly representative specimen are briefly as follows: each of the two drums composing the roller is four inches short of six feet in diameter and is built of heavy oak planking attached to stout iron wheels at either end. These wheels consist of 22 spokes each and a four-inch-wide iron rim to which 40 pieces of 5½ x 3¼ inch oak surfacing stock are attached. The great seat above the drums swung on a frame of massive 3 x 7½ inch mortised oak timbers, all of which pivoted on a central iron axle. It is by no means an overstatement to say that they were contraptions of ponderous bulk and no light weight. This roller cost about $50.

As each drum is five feet wide and the two are separated from each other by a gap of a little over 12 inches, it may be seen that a swath of about 11 feet was made along the road.

Two or three pairs of horses were generally used to draw the roller, although one old photograph that we have shows four pairs, this being a heavy roller or an occasion following an especially severe storm.

Columbia, New Hampshire, another town early to acquire a snow-roller, did so in 1908, and the general satisfaction that resulted led most of the surrounding towns to follow suit. In that year, 20 miles of road in the east part of Columbia were let out on a contract rolling job for the

Birch trees up to six feet in diameter...

Here's a well preserved snow-roller photographed in Dunbarton, New Hampshire, in 1946. The author's son is aboard.

sum of $100—another gentle reminder of our changing monetary standards!

All of the snow-roller drivers with whom we have discussed the virtues of these reminders of the immediate past agree that, although they produced a pretty fair surface for sleighing, and certainly were an improvement over the more primitive methods previously existing, they were not without their drawbacks. With a light, "dry" snow the rollers functioned at their best, but with heavy, wet snow some trouble was entailed with the sticking of the snow to the drums. And when the spring thaws set in, it was all too evident that "the evil men do lives long after them." During the course of a hard winter, the snow in drifted spots would have been firmly packed to a depth of 10 to 12 feet, and having been rolled and rerolled many times the snow was consolidated to an almost icy hardness. Consequently it was often necessary to run a harrow over the roads in early spring to speed up the action of the sun. And when the snow did melt in earnest, for a few days or weeks the country thoroughfares must have presented the aspect of a sort of slushy quagmire, whence the poignant phrase "slump time" for this season.

It may be readily appreciated that the fate of the snow-roller was sealed by the growing popularity of the automobile, although many rollers were in use in rural districts as late as 1935. Nevertheless, for over 50 years, the snow-roller served as a unique, picturesque, and highly distinctive weapon against the annual struggle with New England winter weather. END

Bubble, Bubble, Sing and Stir

by Eliza St. Clair

The ritual of country apple butter boiling is almost a forgotten art...

The taste of apple butter on hot biscuits always recalls to my mind the autumn ritual of an old-time country apple butter boiling. It is then that apples lie on the ground in piles like jewels. Then too, crisp nights, a soft autumn haze, and reluctant sunny days spread themselves across the tapestried landscape.

Several days before the boiling, the horses and wagons would collect the apples and carry them to the cider presses where the topaz nectar would come gushing out into the large barrels. How sweet and spicy the cider tasted!

In the evening, neighbors, friends, and relatives would gather in the farm kitchen. Armed with paring knives, the women would peel and quarter the ripe apples, filling several tubs for the morning boil. The men swapped stories; the children played games; and usually someone played the parlor organ, while everyone sang. And the refreshments! Home-churned ice cream! Cake! And pie! Food for the gods!

The next morning, fires were started, bright and early, at the "kettle place." Large copper kettles were suspended over an open wood fire, and the sweet cider was boiled down to a certain consistency. Then the apples from the tubs were added, and the stirring started. The stir was an oar-like wooden spatula, about 2½ feet long, with a forehandle seven or eight feet long, so one could stand back from the heat of the fire.

The bubbling and stirring continued for most of the day, until the apples were thoroughly cooked. Then sugar and spices were added—plus more bubbling and stirring. Then came the tasting! When it reached the peak of perfection, the kettles were removed from the fire, and the hot, fragrant "butter" was ladled into earthenware crocks for winter use. When it cooled, a thin film of paraffin was poured over the tops of the crocks to seal them. Then the crocks were stored in the pantry or cellar until needed.

How marvelous it tasted on thick hot slices of buttered, home-baked bread . . . or with cottage cheese . . . or on buckwheat cakes at breakfast time on cold winter mornings!

Today when I taste commercially produced apple butter, nostalgia weaves a magic pattern, and memory wafts me in flight. I see again the gleaming brass kettles, with the blazing coals of fire beneath them. I smell again the spicy fragrance in the autumn air, and my mind recalls the gentle, unhurried stirring. My memory adds many ingredients the commercial manufacturer never added—the friendly neighbors, the gossip, the children's laughter, and the singing around the parlor organ!

The ritual of country apple butter boiling is almost a forgotten art, but to me—once a young girl on a farm—it is a cherished memory!   END

APPLE BUTTER

Above: *Peeled and quartered apples ("snits") are added to the boiled-down cider in the kettle.* **Below:** *Apple butter calls for gentle, unhurried, day-long stirring. Emeral B. Jones of Wethersfield, Connecticut, wields the "stir."*

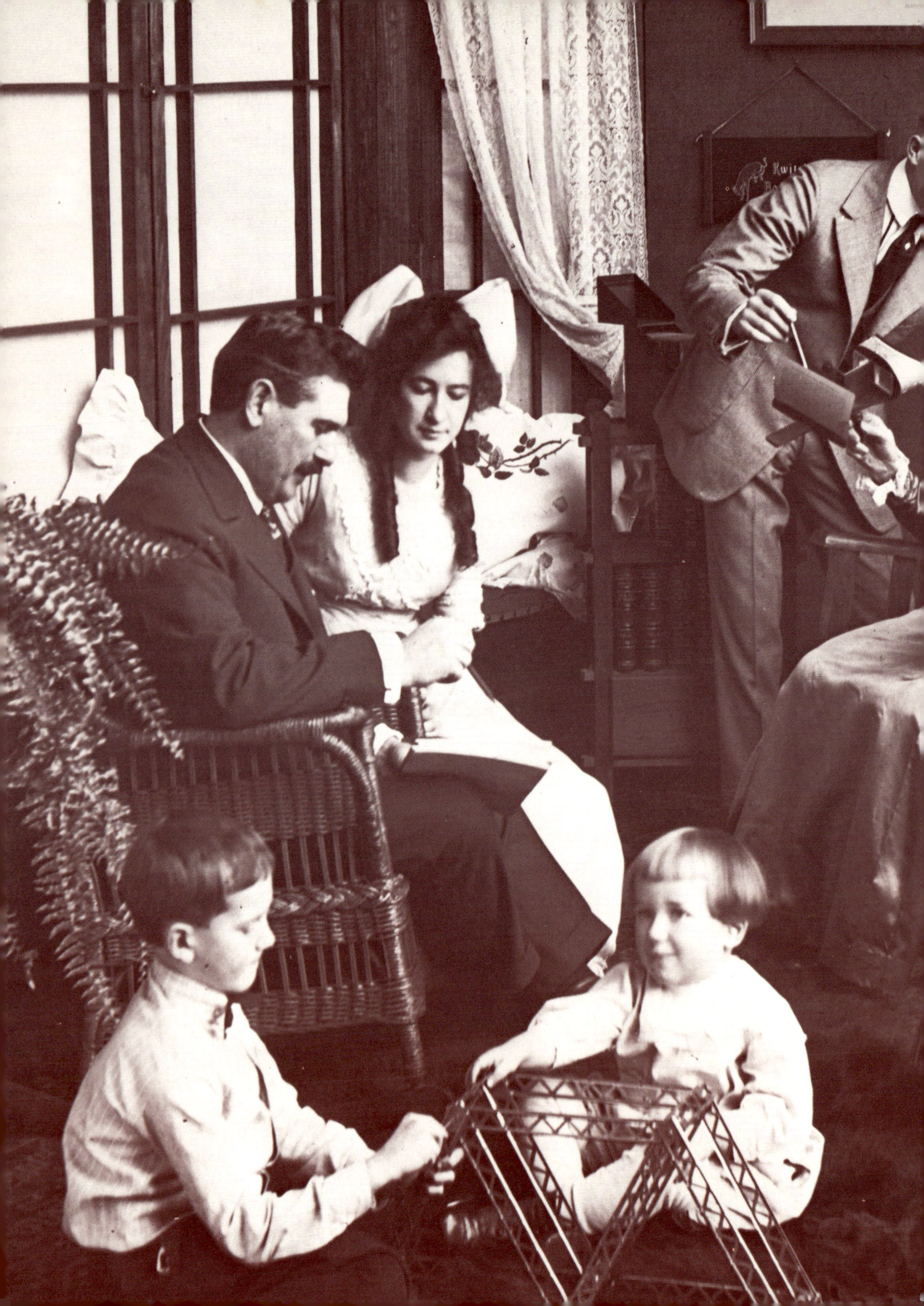

STEREOGRAPHS

Why It's Like You're Right There!

by Paul J. Reale

... the stereoscope occupied the place of honor in every fashionable American parlor.

The minuscule White Mountains community of Littleton, New Hampshire, was the picture entertainment capital of the world at one time, flourishing and famous decades before the emergence of Hollywood with its flickers. For this distinction, savored for nearly a half century, the village had a couple of photo-pioneering hometowners to thank—the full-bearded, Scottish-descent brothers Ben and Ed Kilburn. When Cecil B. De Mille was still a toddler being reared in Ashfield, Massachusetts, the Kilburns were already widely celebrated producers, leaders in the business. And as Littleton was the launching site for the long string of Kilburn smash-hits, the Ammonoosuc River town—population something short of 4,000—ranked unchallenged as the center of the picture industry. Littletonians labored at a multitude of production tasks, and occasionally these chores involved a stint before the cameras. The townspeople could hardly have been aware of it at the time, but history had chosen to include them on its roster of early American "picture stars."

The pictures were stereographs, also known as three-dimensional views or twin-image cards. Between the late 1860s and the first years of the 20th century, in that placid time predating

This photo provided by the Keystone View Co. shows a young man working his way through college by selling "stereos" to a family in the Gay Nineties.

167

rapid transportation and swift communication, the cards were the craze. They lacked sound or motion, but that bothered nobody. It was enough that you could transform a twin-image into a breath-taking, real-as-life scene simply by slipping it into a stereoscope, the hand-held viewer contrived in 1859 by Oliver Wendell Holmes, of all people—the physician, poet, and essayist from Cambridge, Massachusetts. Largely because of his efforts, the stereoscope occupied a place of honor in every fashionable American parlor. For enjoyment and edification, you turned to the 'scope and "stereos," very much as you do the television set and the movies today. Yesterday's TV "specials," living-color film spectaculars, and newsreels were Littleton pictures, streaming forth by the thousands daily in the town's Show Business heyday.

How delightful it was indeed, the family together of an evening, oohing and aahing over the stereographs. The pictures covered a wide variety of subjects, from current events to comedy, from politics to travel, and from romance to religious inspiration.

'Scope to their eyes, citizens sized up the candidates for the United States presidency and then looked in on the victor and his wife in the White House. Americans were transported to distant lands to gape at such marvels as St. Peter's and the pyramids. Views of the Great Chicago Fire (1871) and the Johnstown Flood (1889) helped keep citizens abreast of the news. With Kilburn cards, the nation in 1901 tearfully witnessed in great detail the funeral of President William McKinley, assassinated by the anarchist Leon Czolgosz. Kilburn pictures also put a smile on American faces. Menfolk, for example, smirked at the scene in which a wife, in the thick of heated debate with her husband, shakes a finger at him to expound: "I tell you, woman's suffrage would strengthen the solar plexus of the world!"

"Stereos" were purchased in stationery shops, department stores, and in book emporiums, the price ranging from 25 to 50 cents apiece. Young men working their way through college canvassed the countryside by bike and buggy each summer, selling the pictures. Recruited and trained by the company, a student was not only qualified to explain the principles underlying the merchandise, he was also quite anxious to do so, particularly since this might help spur a fat sale.

As he told it, the three-dimensional illusion hinged on the use of a binocular camera. Having two lenses, one 2½ inches from the other, the apparatus could "see" an image very much as the human eyes do, from two slightly different points of view. Two negatives provide a pair of nearly identical pictures. Mounted in the 'scope, these twin images are translated by the eyes and mind of the viewer into a single, composite scene, with depth and perspective. Just like the farmer said as he peered at a scene: "Why, it's like you're right there, smack dab in the middle of the picture!"

The Kilburns occasionally put together a package of 10 or 12 storytelling scenes. Such a production was "Courtship and Wedding," a sequence popular especially with the marriage-minded.

In this "special," the hero, smartly togged and mustachioed, courts a girl-next-door-type heroine. In proper time, he proposes in the grand manner, a knee on the floor, hands cupping the heart. The gentleman subsequently begs for and is granted her daddy's consent, whereupon the lady shows up in a dazzling white bridal outfit for the solemn church nuptials. There is a going-away feast, the newlyweds attended by kin and closest friends, before the climactic, show-stopping, eye-popping "Alone! Alone at Last!" In this scene, the honeymooners are ensconced in a posh hotel suite, everything first-rate, replete with oriental rugs and fat pots of fan palms. And though the bride is still fully attired, she is plainly letting her hair down. For there she is, parked on the groom's lap, and they are in fact smooching! (It was enough to knock the sensitive viewer clean off the velveteen settee.)

Literary works were sometimes the inspiration for a series. The Kilburns produced, for example, "The Night Before Christmas," based on the Clement C. Moore poem, and "Vision of Sir Launfal," by James Russell Lowell. Extravaganzas of this calibre entailed considerable expense, obviously, what with costuming, props, and sets. Fortunately for the producers, casting was never financially traumatic. Littletonians were only too glad to contribute their thespian abilities to the cause, gratis apparently. A number of them seemed to have

Courtesy Keystone View Co.

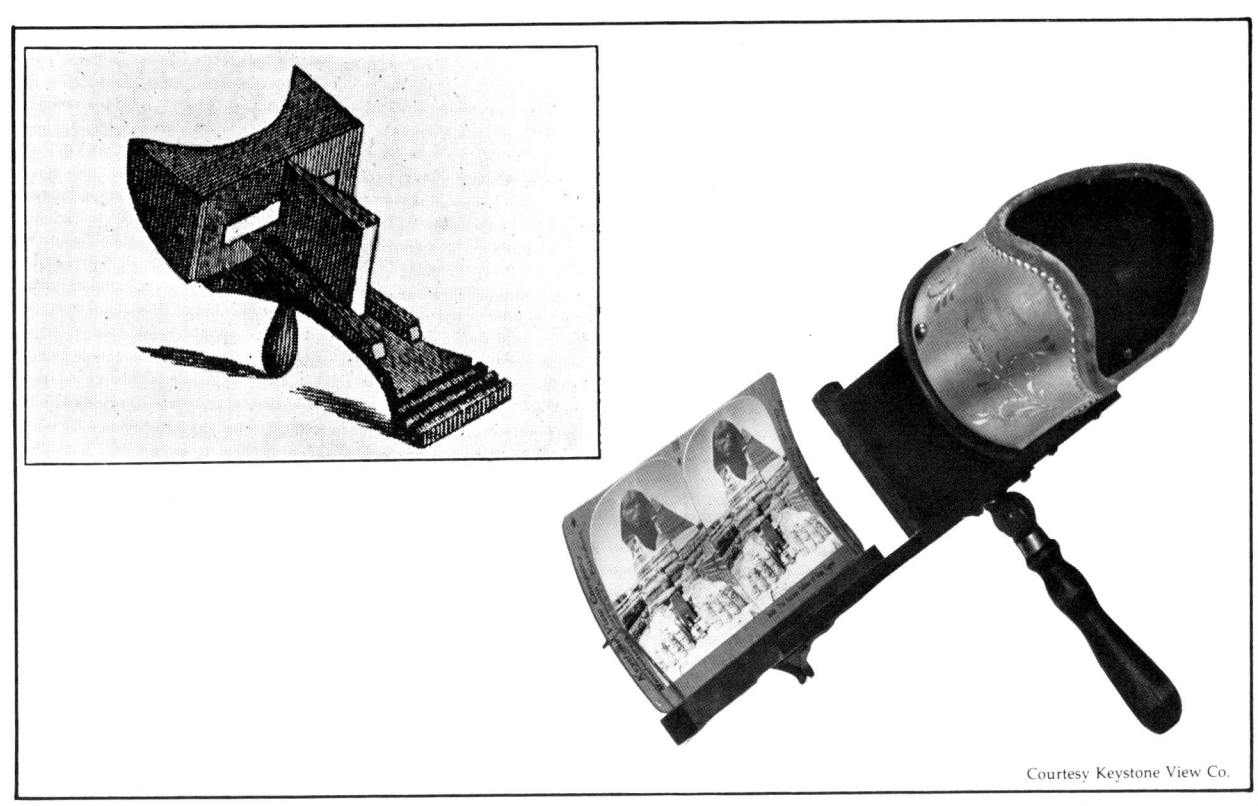

Above left — *the original stereoscope designed by Oliver Wendell Holmes in 1859.* **Right** — *A parlor stereoscope of the '90s, product of the Keystone View Co.* **Below:** *The Kilburn View Shop Manufactory on Cottage Street in Littleton, New Hampshire. Still standing, it is now an apartment house.*

169

Above: *This scenic view is entitled (in five languages, Russian included) "Fathoming the Depth of the Grand Canyon, Arizona, U.S.A." Information about the canyon is printed on the back, along with a bibliography of pertinent literature.* **Below:** *Haying — a family photo made into a stereograph. "Harry holding the horse, Joe on top. Uncle by side of cart."*

performed with some regularity, playing one role and then another. With close observation, the viewer sees, for example, Santa Claus showing up in "Courtship and Wedding" festivities, and the Other Woman in "Things Seen and Not Seen" is the happily married wife in "Last in Bed Put Out the Lights."

If the players couldn't expect pay, they couldn't expect their names in lights either, or even on the cards. There was, after all, just so much room on a stereograph. In front, just below the twin-photos, appeared a caption describing the business afoot or spelling out the words being uttered by the principals. As to the card's backside, that was territory practically out-of-bounds to anything except that all-important message, the statement that was guaranteeing the town a place in the sun. In large scrawling letters, the message said: "Photographed and Published by Kilburn Brothers . . . Littleton, N.H."

Benjamin West Kilburn (1827-1909) and Edward (1830-1884) were the sons of Josiah Kilburn, pillar of the Littleton Congregational Church, zealous temperance leader, and proprietor of an iron foundry. The boys aided their father at the shop until Ed, smitten by the promising new art craft that people were calling "photography," apprenticed himself to O. C. Bolton, owner of an attic studio downtown in Littleton.

The pupil purchased the business eventually,

Two views in the current events category. **Above:** *Commodore Schley's flagship* Brooklyn, *of the "Flying Squadron," U.S. Navy.* **Below:** *"Ruins of the Great Fire, Haverhill, Mass., Feb. 17 and 18, 1882."*

and Ben was persuaded to team up as partner. Judging by the look of things, little coaxing was necessary. Townspeople, long aware of Ben's enthusiasm for hunting and fishing, observed that while he continued to drive his wagon into the hills every opportunity, the nature of his cargo had changed dramatically. Instead of tackle and firearms, the hardy outdoorsman lugged a camera, plus a rather strange and unwieldly assortment of photographic equipment. (In photography's infancy, a cameraman away from his studio was obliged to "shoot" his picture and process it on the spot. His paraphernalia therefore had to include glass negative plates, chemicals, and a black-lined tent for use as a darkroom.)

Ben was quick to master the intricacies of stereoscopic picture-making. What he "bagged" on his excursions were the scenes that were to start him and his brother up the road to photographic renown. There was gold as well as game in the hills of home. Ben's mountain pictures drew raves—and buyers. The demand for the scenes was lively, the one of the Old Man of the Mountain at Franconia Notch being a big favorite.

The business was founded in 1866, following the return of the brothers from service in the Civil War. The partnership was a practically ideal one. Ben and Ed were men of good habits, with initiative and imagination. They were religious people, and in marriage they were

Courtesy Frank L. Flay

Courtesy Paul A. Darling

Left: "Morning Glories." On the back, the photographer, R.B. Lewis of Hudson, Mass., announced unblushingly — "A PHOTOGRAPHIC FEAT UNPARALLELED," and goes on to explain that "The photographing of so many babies in one group, and getting them ALL STILL is a thing probably never before accomplished!" **Right:** A halcyon moment labeled "American Scenery, Miscellaneous."

happy. (Ben wed Caroline L. Burnham of Bethlehem, New Hampshire, in 1853. Ed married a Littleton teacher, Adaline S. Owen of St. Johnsbury, Vermont, in 1857.) Ben was endowed with immense energy, a rich sense of humor, and the facility for making many friends. Of cosmopolitan mien, he could feel as much at home in any of the world's capitals as in his own village. In many ways, his talents were complementary to Ed's. The younger brother was less robust, more reserved. His métier was clearly management and merchandising. The arrangement whereby Ben took the pictures and Ed "kept the store" seemed foreordained.

Encouraged by the success of the mountain scenes, Ben expanded his field to give the public pictures of Washington, D.C., Niagara Falls, and San Francisco, before moving on to Mexico.

"Kilburn Brothers are overrun with business," the *White Mountain Republic* let it be known upon Ben's return to Littleton. "With their liveliest work, they are unable to fill orders as fast as they come in. Their Mexican views are just being put on the market, and the demand for them is great . . ."

The Kilburn Brothers' business was booming most assuredly, even while many hundreds of other photographers took to the field to capitalize on stereoscopy's soaring popularity.

From cramped attic quarters, the brothers moved into the whole of another building, only to find in 1872 that this, too, could no longer contain their burgeoning operations. The next year, therefore, they occupied a commodious four-story building on Cottage Street, a structure that stands to this day, now as the Kilburn Apartments, home of a number of families. In 1873 this was the Kilburn View Shop, largest concern of its kind in the world. Its output was a phenomenal 2,000 to 5,000 views a day, when small firms were managing 200.

The enthusiastic reception given the Mexican views suggested to Ed that Americans might welcome just as heartily scenes of other foreign lands, particularly since no other company had yet undertaken such a project. Agreeing that the sales potential did exist, the older brother packed and hastened forth. Ben, or "B. W." as he was now known, traversed the British Isles, Europe, Greece, Egypt, and the Holy Land, repeating many hundreds of times his photographic ritual.

A decision made as to the scene he wanted to film, Ben carefully poured a syrupy collodion-potassium iodide mixture over a glass negative plate and allowed the plate to become "tacky." Satisfied that the coating was smooth and free of air bubbles, he immersed the plate in a silver nitrate solution, thereby rendering it light sensitive. The "wet" plate was inserted in the camera and exposed, then developed in Pyrogallic acid, fixed in "hyposulfite of soda," washed, and packaged for shipment home.

In the View Shop, the job of manufacturing "stereos" from the negative fell to a staff of nearly 100 persons. In the strongly daylighted upper floors, men positioned the negatives against freshly albuminized paper and strung them in frames in windows. Pictures derived by "sun-printing" were carried downstairs to ladies who scissored the prints to proper size, brushed thick mucilage across their backs, and mounted them on cards measuring 7 x 3½ inches. The printer applied caption material with a handpress and passed the cards along to the inspectors.

The Kilburns scored again with their foreign views, pictures to whet the wanderlust. The You-Are-There realism of the scenes delighted armchair travelers and, in fact, caused their number to multiply. Sales rocketed, and other stereoscopic firms snapped into action. They sent cameramen scurrying abroad, over the trail blazed by Ben.

Still breaking new paths, the View Shop introduced the "warped" or curved look, an innovation engineered to accentuate the three-dimensional illusion of heretofore flatmount cards. Patent rights did not restrain the competition. Within a few years the "warped" card was every company's property.

When not "on location," Ben was busy at home, organizing townspeople as performers in the pictures that have since come to be known as the "sentimentals." These depicted the blessings and the bruises of domesticity. They were scenes calculated to evoke laughter, yearning, and tears. In these productions, children fondle pets, play with toys, recite bedside prayers, wage pillow fights. A mother sorrows at a child's grave. In "Meeting the Board of Education," a father picks his errant son off the floor by the seat of the pants to drive home a lesson with a properly placed plank. Aware that a mouse has invaded the bedroom, a wife rattles her husband awake, bounds from the bed to the chair, hoists her nightie well above her knees, and shrieks: "The monster! Be brave if you love me, Jack!"

For some scenes in the category, "sentimentals" would seem something of a misnomer. They border on the risqué. A shoe salesman fits shoes on the well-formed legs of a lady in a scene titled simply: "Don't Get Above Your Business." "Girls, I hear rats!" cries a coed to her roommates, all of them occupying a bed under which had slipped two collegians. (In the subsequent scene, the coeds swiftly evict the intruders with brooms.)

A Littleton septuagenarian, Mrs. Charles E. Keyes, and another town resident, Mrs. William E. Wallace, in her 80s, reminisced in 1965 as to how it was.

In the main, performers were recruited from among Kilburn friends and View Shop employees, said Mrs. Keyes, also recalling that "cousins of mine and even the family dog" were called upon to emote. As a high school girl, Mrs. Keyes worked summers at the shop. In later years she was a teacher. Her husband, Charlie, was a View Shop artist-photographer.

Mrs. Wallace was something of a "child star," summoned before the camera so often that "I resolved that if I ever could do as I wanted, I never would be in any more pictures."

In her case, the photographer was not Ben Kilburn but her father, William E. Bellows, a partner with his brother George in the Littleton View Company, a small-scale but lucrative enterprise existent 1883 to 1900, reportedly as a successor to the F. G. Weller business started in 1866.

"The performers were not paid, not that I ever heard about," Mrs. Wallace volunteered.

Weller, whose avocation was music, bowed out of the picture after a highly successful career that helped strengthen the town's reputation as the stereoscopic entertainment capital. Weller's forte were "sentimentals" and avant garde productions. Pioneering in "trick" pho-

Above: *"Girls, I hear rats!" In this scene from a Kilburn story-telling package, Littletonians enact a little drama which ends with the two collegian intruders being evicted with brooms.*

tography, he created visions and fantasies peopled by cherubs and ghosts. In addition, he attempted series based on literary works, one of these being "Manfred," inspired by Lord Byron's dramatic poem. Weller and the Kilburns were the only American companies to undertake such projects.

* * * * *

At the View Shop, employees started work at 7 A.M., ate home-packed lunches on the premises, and departed at 5 P.M. Their weekly earnings ranged from $2.50 to $5.00, a tidy sum in those days. And nobody could say that Ed wasn't a fine boss. Occasionally shedding his reserve, the gentlemanly Ed would sail into the place and organize a "sing," he himself contributing a strong melodic baritone to the happy proceedings. Once, it is told, he barged in and, suppressing a grin, ordered everybody out—to a "sugaring-off" party.

When Ed retired in 1877 to devote his final years to his large farm, Ben was left to manage the shop, first alone, and then with the aid of his daughter Caroline and her husband, the lawyer Daniel C. Remich. Tied down as he was to business and to a growing number of civic duties, "B. W." was able to return to his camera only rarely. Typically, company representatives were assigned to take the pictures, and the desirable work of "freelancers" was purchased. In this way Kilburn continued to inform and amuse America, and the number of individual views bearing the Kilburn imprint—1,105 in 1873—swelled beyond 100,000.

These "stereos" show the Wild West and the Indians, railroads starting to span the nation, Negro life in Dixie, and ladies clad in billowing black "bathing" costumes as they frolic in the Atlantic City surf.

Ben did not neglect the American appetite for

Above: "An Effectual Remedy;" this F.G. Weller "sentimental" could almost be a Saturday Evening Post cover.
Right: Elaborate costumes and scenery distinguish this Kilburn extravaganza.

news, for there are pictures of tornadoes, fires, floods, and fairs. The View Shop was "official photographer" for the Columbian World's Fair in Chicago in 1892-3 and as such took 15,000 negatives, up to that time a record number of pictures for a single event.

The Klondike Gold Rush (1898) was stereoscopized, and Kilburn cameramen pictured John Philip Sousa leading his band up Broadway in a frenzied salute to Commander George Dewey, hero of the Battle of Manila Bay (1899). Kilburn coverage of the McKinley obsequies was so complete that viewers even saw the surgical table on which the President's gun wounds were tended.

* * * * *

As often as he could, Mrs. Keyes's husband went to Ben's house to read to the aged employer or to take him out in the wheelchair, sometimes past the Kilburn Elementary School put up in 1894. Charlie took "B. W." to the View Shop only when the old man insisted on going there. It was better that Ben, in failing health, not concern himself too much any more with the business that had come upon slump times.

"Charlie," his widow remembered, "remained until the doors were closed."

The doors closed soon after Ben's death at 82. The Kilburn negatives passed into the hands of the Keystone View Company of Meadville, Pennsylvania (now the Keystone Division of the Mast Development Corp., located in Davenport, Iowa). "I sold thousands of views to the junk dealer," said Mrs. Wallace, recalling the onset of a new age. Americans were stuffing their 'scopes and "stereos" into the attic or the trash barrel so as to give full attention to sputtering automobiles, safe-conduct passenger trains, do-it-yourself box cameras and, of course, moving pictures.

END

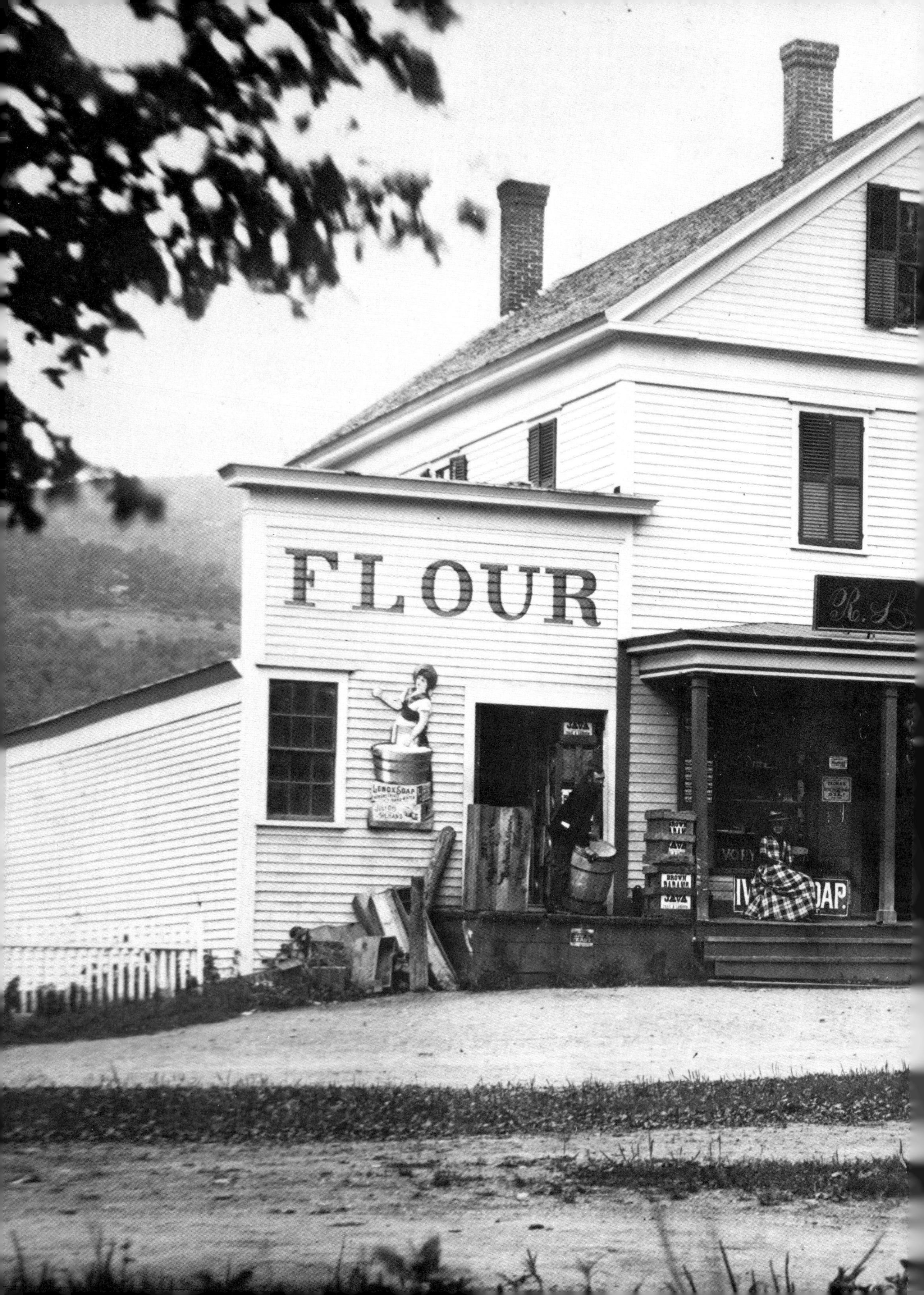
FLOUR
LENOX SOAP